TABLE OF CONTENTS

BREAKFAST DELIGHTS

SOUPS AND STEWS

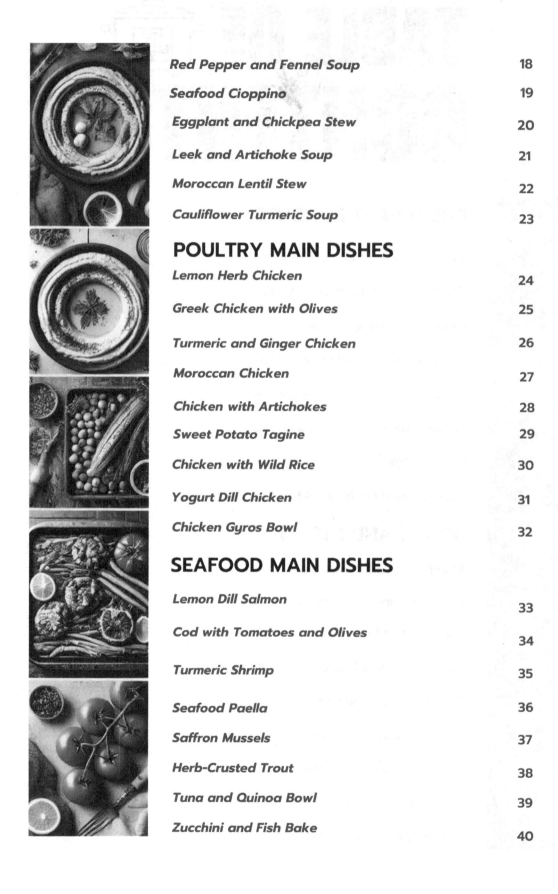

POULTRY MAIN DISHES

SEAFOOD MAIN DISHES

PLANT-BASED MAIN DISHES

SIDE DISHES

SNACKS AND APPETIZERS

MEAL PLANS

Healthiest Crock Pot Recipes in the Planet

CCooking doesn't have to be complicated, and eating healthy shouldn't feel like a chore. Welcome to the ultimate guide for embracing the Mediterranean diet with the ease of a crockpot. This book is your key to unlocking flavorful, wholesome meals that promote health, reduce inflammation, and simplify your life. Whether you're looking to adopt healthier habits, support your well-being, or just make dinner easier, you're in the right place.

Forget about spending hours in the kitchen or dealing with mountains of dishes. These recipes are designed to be simple, stress-free, and packed with the vibrant, bold flavors of the Mediterranean. Think tender braised vegetables, hearty stews, protein-packed legumes, and dishes bursting with the goodness of olive oil, fresh herbs, and zesty citrus. Your crockpot does the heavy lifting—just toss in the ingredients, set it, and savor the results.

This book isn't about gourmet techniques or exotic ingredients; it's about accessible, approachable meals that nourish your body and delight your taste buds. Whether you're new to cooking or a seasoned pro, these recipes fit seamlessly into your lifestyle. Perfect for weeknight dinners, meal prep, or sharing with loved ones, they're as versatile as they are delicious.

If you're ready to eat well without the hassle, this book is your starting point. Dive into the Mediterranean way of life with recipes that support heart health, fight inflammation, and celebrate natural, wholesome ingredients. With your crockpot as your trusty partner, creating incredible meals has never been easier. Let's get cooking—your health (and taste buds) will thank you!

"Let food be Thy medicine and medicine be Thy food."

– Hippocrates

Mediterranean Veggie Frittata

INGREDIENTS

- 4 large eggs
- 1 cup fresh spinach
- 8 cherry tomatoes
- 1 tbsp olive oil
- 1 tsp dried oregano

WHY IS IT GREAT?

This Mediterranean Veggie Frittata is not just delicious but also anti-inflammatory and perfectly suited for crock pot cooking! The olive oil provides monounsaturated fats that fight inflammation, while spinach and cherry tomatoes are loaded with antioxidants like vitamin C, beta-carotene, and flavonoids to reduce oxidative stress. Oregano offers natural compounds that amplify anti-inflammatory benefits. Using a crock pot enhances these qualities by preserving nutrients through slow, gentle cooking, ensuring the ingredients retain their health-boosting properties. It's also a hands-free way to prepare the dish, making it ideal for busy lifestyles. This gluten-free, vegetarian recipe is highly versatile—easily adaptable with seasonal vegetables. Serve it as a hearty breakfast or pair with a fresh salad for a light, nourishing meal packed with vibrant flavors and health benefits!

PREPARATION

- Coat the crock pot with 1 tbsp olive oil to prevent sticking.
- In a bowl, whisk 4 large eggs with salt, pepper, and 1 tsp dried oregano.
- Place 1 cup fresh spinach into the crock pot, spreading it evenly at the base.
- Halve 8 cherry tomatoes and layer them over the spinach.
- Pour the egg mixture gently into the crock pot, ensuring the veggies are covered.
- Cover and cook on low for 2–3 hours until the frittata is set and firm.
- Garnish with fresh herbs and a lemon wedge before serving hot.

NUTRITION

Per serving: calories 220, protein 12g, total fat 16g (saturated fat 4g, monounsaturated fat 10g, polyunsaturated fat 2g), carbohydrates 6g (fiber 2g, sugars 3g, added sugars 0g), cholesterol 0mg, sodium 220mg, potassium 300mg, calcium 70mg, iron 1.5mg, magnesium 30mg, Vitamin A 600µg, Vitamin C 15mg, Vitamin D 2µg, Vitamin E 2mg, Vitamin K 120µg, Omega-3 0.1g, Omega-6 0.3g. Glycemic load is low, net carbs 4g. This gluten-free, vegetarian recipe contains no nuts or shellfish, making it suitable for most diets.

Golden Quinoa Breakfast Bowl

INGREDIENTS

- 1/2 cup quinoa
- 1 cup almond milk
- 1/2 tsp turmeric
- 1 tbsp honey
- 1/2 cup mixed berries

WHY IS IT GREAT?

This Golden Quinoa Breakfast Bowl is a nutritious way to start your day! Turmeric, a powerful anti-inflammatory spice, supports joint health and reduces inflammation, while quinoa provides complete protein and fiber for lasting energy. Almond milk and honey add a creamy sweetness without dairy, and fresh berries are rich in antioxidants and vitamins. Cooking this in a crock pot enhances the recipe's flavors and texture by slow-cooking the quinoa until it's tender and infused with turmeric. The crock pot also makes this dish hassle-free, perfect for busy mornings or meal prep. Garnish with extra turmeric or mint for a pop of color. Enjoy this warm, wholesome bowl that's both visually stunning and packed with anti-inflammatory, nutrient-dense goodness!

PREPARATION

- Coat the crock pot with 1 tbsp olive oil to prevent sticking.
- In a bowl, whisk 4 large eggs with salt, pepper, and 1 tsp dried oregano.
- Place 1 cup fresh spinach into the crock pot, spreading it evenly at the base.
- Halve 8 cherry tomatoes and layer them over the spinach.
- Pour the egg mixture gently into the crock pot, ensuring the veggies are covered.
- Cover and cook on low for 2–3 hours until the frittata is set and firm.
- Garnish with fresh herbs and a lemon wedge before serving hot.

NUTRITION

Per serving: calories 210, protein 6g, total fat 4g (saturated fat 0g, monounsaturated fat 2g, polyunsaturated fat 2g), carbohydrates 40g (fiber 5g, sugars 12g, added sugars 6g), cholesterol 0mg, sodium 40mg, potassium 300mg, calcium 100mg, iron 1.8mg, magnesium 60mg, Vitamin A 10µg, Vitamin C 15mg, Vitamin D 0µg, Vitamin E 4mg, Vitamin K 10µg, Omega-3 0.1g, Omega-6 0.2g. Glycemic load is moderate, net carbs 35g. This recipe is gluten-free and dairy-free, suitable for vegan diets. Contains nuts (almond milk), so not suitable for those with nut allergies.

Lemon-Blueberry Oatmeal

INGREDIENTS

- 1/2 cup steel-cut oats
- 1 cup almond milk
- 1/2 cup blueberries
- 1 tbsp honey
- 1 tsp lemon zest

WHY IS IT GREAT?

This Crockpot Lemon-Blueberry Oatmeal is the perfect way to start your day with an anti-inflammatory boost! Blueberries are rich in antioxidants that combat inflammation, while steel-cut oats provide fiber to support heart health and steady energy levels. Lemon zest adds a refreshing, vitamin-packed tang that brightens the dish. The crock pot enhances the recipe by gently cooking the oats to creamy perfection while infusing the flavors of blueberries and lemon throughout. This hands-free method is ideal for busy mornings or meal prep. Add a drizzle of honey for natural sweetness and garnish beautifully for a visually appealing and nourishing dish. With its balance of flavors, nutrients, and ease, this oatmeal is as wholesome as it is delicious—great for breakfast or a hearty snack!

PREPARATION

- Combine 1/2 cup steel-cut oats and 1 cup almond milk in the crock pot. Stir to mix evenly.
- Add 1/2 cup blueberries and 1 tsp lemon zest for a burst of flavor. Stir gently.
- Cook on low for 4–6 hours, ensuring the oats are tender and creamy.
- Stir in 1 tbsp honey just before serving for sweetness and flavor enhancement.
- Garnish with extra blueberries, lemon zest, and a drizzle of honey for visual appeal.
- Serve warm directly from the crock pot, ensuring all toppings are evenly distributed.
- Enjoy this hearty, aromatic oatmeal that's packed with flavor and nourishment.

NUTRITION

Per serving: calories 230, protein 6g, total fat 4g (saturated fat 0g, monounsaturated fat 2g, polyunsaturated fat 2g), carbohydrates 45g (fiber 6g, sugars 14g, added sugars 6g), cholesterol 0mg, sodium 40mg, potassium 240mg, calcium 150mg, iron 1.5mg, magnesium 50mg, Vitamin A 10µg, Vitamin C 5mg, Vitamin D 0µg, Vitamin E 3mg, Vitamin K 10µg, Omega-3 0.1g, Omega-6 0.2g. Glycemic load is moderate, net carbs 39g. This recipe is gluten-free and dairy-free, suitable for vegetarian diets. Contains nuts (almond milk), making it unsuitable for those with nut allergies.

Sweet Potato and Turmeric Hash

INGREDIENTS

- 2 cups sweet potatoes (diced)
- 1 cup bell peppers (diced)
- 1 tbsp olive oil
- 1 tsp turmeric
- 2 tbsp parsley (chopped)

WHY IS IT GREAT?

Sweet Potato and Turmeric Hash is a vibrant, anti-inflammatory dish bursting with flavor! Sweet potatoes are packed with beta-carotene and fiber, promoting eye and gut health. Turmeric adds a golden color and anti-inflammatory properties, helping reduce inflammation and supporting overall wellness. Bell peppers contribute antioxidants and Vitamin C, enhancing the dish's nutritional value. Cooking it in a crock pot enhances the flavors while keeping the sweet potatoes tender and perfectly cooked. This hands-off method saves time and locks in nutrients. Garnished with fresh parsley, this dish is as visually appealing as it is wholesome. Ideal as a side dish or a light meal, it pairs beautifully with grilled proteins or a simple salad. Its balance of health benefits and convenience makes it a winning choice!

PREPARATION

- Peel and dice 2 cups sweet potatoes and dice 1 cup bell peppers.
- Add sweet potatoes and bell peppers to the crock pot. Drizzle with 1 tbsp olive oil.
- Sprinkle 1 tsp turmeric evenly over the vegetables and mix gently to coat.
- Cook on low for 4–5 hours or until the sweet potatoes are tender.
- Stir occasionally to ensure even cooking and flavor distribution.
- Garnish with 2 tbsp chopped parsley before serving for a fresh touch.
- Serve hot directly from the crock pot, ideal as a side dish or a light meal.

NUTRITION

Per serving: calories 180, protein 2g, total fat 7g (saturated fat 1g, monounsaturated fat 5g, polyunsaturated fat 1g), carbohydrates 28g (fiber 4g, sugars 6g, added sugars 0g), cholesterol 0mg, sodium 50mg, potassium 500mg, calcium 40mg, iron 1.2mg, magnesium 30mg, Vitamin A 800μg, Vitamin C 50mg, Vitamin D 0μg, Vitamin E 1mg, Vitamin K 20μg, Omega-3 0.1g, Omega-6 0.3g. Glycemic load is moderate, net carbs 24g. This gluten-free, vegan recipe is nut-free, making it suitable for most diets.

Warm Pear and Walnut Compote

INGREDIENTS

- 2 pears (sliced)
- 1/4 cup walnuts (chopped)
- 1 tbsp honey
- 1 tsp cinnamon
- 1 tbsp lemon juice

WHY IS IT GREAT?

Warm Pear and Walnut Compote is a comforting, anti-inflammatory treat perfect for any time of the day! Pears provide natural sweetness and fiber, supporting digestion and stabilizing blood sugar. Walnuts add crunch and omega-3 fatty acids, which are known for their anti-inflammatory benefits. Cinnamon enhances the flavor while also contributing antioxidants and helping to regulate blood sugar. The crock pot is ideal for this recipe as it allows the pears to soften gently, infusing the flavors of honey and spices without requiring constant attention. This hands-free method retains nutrients and creates an aromatic, tender compote. Serve it as a wholesome dessert or breakfast topping, with yogurt or oatmeal. Its warm, spiced profile makes it perfect for cozy, nourishing meals!

PREPARATION

- Slice 2 pears and place them in the crock pot.
- Add 1/4 cup chopped walnuts over the pears for added texture.
- Drizzle 1 tbsp honey and sprinkle 1 tsp cinnamon over the mixture.
- Pour 1 tbsp lemon juice to enhance flavor and prevent browning.
- Cook on low for 3–4 hours until pears are tender and aromatic.
- Stir gently before serving to ensure even coating of the spices and honey.
- Serve warm, garnished with extra walnuts or a dollop of yogurt for a creamy touch.

NUTRITION

Per serving: calories 190, protein 2g, total fat 8g (saturated fat 0.5g, monounsaturated fat 2g, polyunsaturated fat 5g), carbohydrates 30g (fiber 5g, sugars 20g, added sugars 6g), cholesterol 0mg, sodium 5mg, potassium 200mg, calcium 30mg, iron 0.8mg, magnesium 25mg, Vitamin A 5µg, Vitamin C 8mg, Vitamin D 0µg, Vitamin E 0.5mg, Vitamin K 4µg, Omega-3 0.2g, Omega-6 0.4g. Glycemic load is moderate, net carbs 25g. This gluten-free, vegetarian recipe contains nuts (walnuts).

Spinach and Tomato Shakshuka

INGREDIENTS

- 4 large eggs
- 2 cups spinach
- 1 cup diced tomatoes
- 1 tbsp olive oil
- 1 tsp paprika

WHY IS IT GREAT?

Spinach and Tomato Shakshuka is a vibrant, anti-inflammatory dish packed with nutrients! Tomatoes and spinach are rich in antioxidants like lycopene and flavonoids that reduce inflammation and support overall health. Paprika adds a smoky depth and contains capsaicin, which further enhances anti-inflammatory benefits. Cooking this in a crock pot ensures the tomatoes and spinach release their natural flavors and maintain their nutritional integrity, while the eggs cook to perfection. This hands-free method is convenient for busy days and locks in moisture for a deliciously tender dish. Serve as a hearty breakfast, brunch, or light dinner with crusty bread or a simple salad. Its flexibility, health benefits, and ease make it a winning recipe for any occasion!

PREPARATION

- Heat 1 tbsp olive oil in the crock pot on the sauté setting, then add 1 cup diced tomatoes.
- Stir in 1 tsp paprika and let the mixture simmer for 5 minutes until aromatic.
- Add 2 cups spinach, gently stirring to combine with the tomato base.
- Crack 4 large eggs on top of the mixture, ensuring even spacing.
- Cover and cook on low for 1–2 hours until eggs are set to your preference.
- Garnish with fresh herbs and a drizzle of olive oil before serving hot.
- Serve directly from the crock pot, ideal with crusty bread or as a light meal.

NUTRITION

Per serving: calories 190, protein 11g, total fat 12g (saturated fat 3g, monounsaturated fat 7g, polyunsaturated fat 2g), carbohydrates 8g (fiber 2g, sugars 4g, added sugars 0g), cholesterol 190mg, sodium 200mg, potassium 350mg, calcium 70mg, iron 2mg, magnesium 30mg, Vitamin A 900µg, Vitamin C 15mg, Vitamin D 2µg, Vitamin E 2mg, Vitamin K 130µg, Omega-3 0.1g, Omega-6 0.3g. Glycemic load is low, net carbs 6g. This gluten-free, vegetarian recipe contains no nuts or shellfish, making it suitable for most diets.

Golden Millet Porridge

INGREDIENTS

- ½ cup millet
- 1 cup almond milk
- ½ tsp cinnamon
- 1 tbsp honey
- ½ tsp fresh grated ginger

WHY IS IT GREAT?

Golden Millet Porridge is a nutritional powerhouse with anti-inflammatory benefits, thanks to ginger and cinnamon. Millet is a gluten-free grain rich in magnesium, ideal for sustaining energy and supporting digestion. The recipe's simplicity makes it a flexible choice for dietary needs—swap almond milk for other plant-based options, and adjust sweeteners for preference. Cooking it in a crock pot is perfect for busy days, allowing flavors to meld beautifully while you focus on other tasks. This dish pairs health and sustainability by using plant-based, whole ingredients. Serve as a comforting breakfast or light dinner. Its presentation is inviting, especially with garnishes like nuts or fruit, and it's a delightful example of how healthy eating can be delicious and fuss-free.

PREPARATION

- Rinse ½ cup of millet under cold water and drain thoroughly.
- Add the millet to the crock pot along with 1 cup of almond milk, 1 cup of water, and ½ tsp of grated ginger.
- Stir in ½ tsp of cinnamon and cover the pot with the lid.
- Set the crock pot to low heat and let the porridge cook gently for 3-4 hours, stirring occasionally.
- When the millet has absorbed most of the liquid, mix in 1 tbsp of honey.
- Serve the porridge warm in bowls, garnished with a drizzle of almond milk, a sprinkle of cinnamon, and fresh ginger slivers.
- Enjoy the creamy and wholesome flavor with optional toppings like nuts or fruit.

NUTRITION

Calories: 180 kcal, Protein: 5 g, Total Fat: 3 g (Saturated: 0.2 g, Monounsaturated: 1.5 g, Polyunsaturated: 0.5 g), Carbohydrates: 33 g (Fiber: 3 g, Sugars: 10 g, Added Sugars: 5 g), Sodium: 60 mg, Potassium: 150 mg, Calcium: 120 mg, Iron: 1.5 mg, Magnesium: 45 mg, Vitamin A: 50 IU, Vitamin C: 1 mg, Vitamin D: 0 IU, Vitamin E: 2 mg, Vitamin K: 2 µg, Vitamin B-complex: 0.3 mg, Omega-3: 0.05 g, Omega-6: 0.4 g, Glycemic Load: 10, Cholesterol: 0 mg, Net Carbs: 30 g.

Zucchini and Herb Breakfast Bake

INGREDIENTS

- 1 cup zucchini, sliced
- 2 eggs
- 1 tbsp olive oil
- ½ tsp oregano
- ¼ tsp black pepper

WHY IS IT GREAT?

This Zucchini and Herb Breakfast Bake is a fantastic way to start your day with a nutrient-packed meal. Zucchini provides essential vitamins and anti-inflammatory properties, while eggs offer protein for sustained energy. The oregano and olive oil add Mediterranean flair, enhancing both flavor and heart health. Crock pot preparation ensures even cooking and makes it stress-free—just set it and go! This recipe is great for meal prep or as a low-carb, gluten-free breakfast. Serving suggestions include pairing with a fresh salad or whole-grain toast for variety. Feel free to substitute spices or add cheese for extra richness. Its light, wholesome appeal and ease of preparation make it a dish you'll love again and again.

PREPARATION

- Lightly oil the crock pot with 1 tbsp of olive oil to prevent sticking.
- Layer 1 cup of thinly sliced zucchini evenly at the bottom.
- In a bowl, whisk 2 eggs with ½ tsp of oregano and ¼ tsp of black pepper.
- Pour the egg mixture over the zucchini layer, ensuring an even spread.
- Set the crock pot on low heat and cook for 2-3 hours, until the eggs are set.
- Check periodically and avoid overcooking to retain the zucchini's texture.
- Serve warm, garnished with fresh oregano or additional black pepper for flavor.

NUTRITION

Calories: 130 kcal, Protein: 7 g, Total Fat: 10 g (Saturated: 2 g, Monounsaturated: 6 g, Polyunsaturated: 2 g), Carbohydrates: 4 g (Fiber: 1 g, Sugars: 2 g, Added Sugars: 0 g), Sodium: 110 mg, Potassium: 200 mg, Calcium: 30 mg, Iron: 1 mg, Magnesium: 15 mg, Vitamin A: 100 IU, Vitamin C: 6 mg, Vitamin D: 15 IU, Vitamin E: 2 mg, Vitamin K: 12 µg, Vitamin B-complex: 0.2 mg, Omega-3: 0.1 g, Omega-6: 0.2 g, Glycemic Load: 2, Cholesterol: 160 mg, Net Carbs: 3 g.Dietary suitability: Gluten-free, low-carb, keto-friendly. Allergen information: Contains eggs.

Mediterranean Lentil Soup

INGREDIENTS

- ½ cup lentils
- 2 cups vegetable broth
- 1 tbsp olive oil
- ½ cup chopped tomatoes
- ½ tsp cumin

WHY IS IT GREAT?

Mediterranean Lentil Soup is a deliciously nourishing dish packed with plant-based protein, fiber, and essential nutrients. Lentils and tomatoes are rich in antioxidants, supporting heart health and reducing inflammation, while cumin aids digestion. It's a versatile recipe that can be customized with your favorite herbs and spices. Cooking this soup in a crock pot enhances its flavors as the ingredients meld over time, making it incredibly rich and aromatic. Serve with crusty bread or a fresh salad for a complete meal. This dish is sustainable, affordable, and great for batch cooking, letting you enjoy wholesome Mediterranean flavors without hassle. Perfect for cozy evenings, the vibrant presentation adds an inviting, heartwarming appeal to your table.

PREPARATION

- Rinse ½ cup of lentils under cold water and set aside.
- In a crock pot, combine ½ cup lentils, 2 cups vegetable broth, and ½ cup chopped tomatoes.
- Stir in ½ tsp cumin and 1 tbsp olive oil for added flavor.
- Set the crock pot to low heat and cook for 4-5 hours, stirring occasionally.
- Check lentils for doneness; they should be soft but not mushy.
- Adjust seasoning with salt or pepper if desired.
- Serve hot, garnished with fresh parsley and a drizzle of olive oil for a wholesome touch.

NUTRITION

Calories: 200 kcal, Protein: 10 g, Total Fat: 5 g (Saturated: 0.7 g, Monounsaturated: 3.2 g, Polyunsaturated: 0.8 g), Carbohydrates: 28 g (Fiber: 6 g, Sugars: 4 g, Added Sugars: 0 g), Sodium: 350 mg, Potassium: 350 mg, Calcium: 40 mg, Iron: 3 mg, Magnesium: 30 mg, Vitamin A: 500 IU, Vitamin C: 8 mg, Vitamin D: 0 IU, Vitamin E: 2 mg, Vitamin K: 15 µg, Vitamin B-complex: 0.4 mg, Omega-3: 0.05 g, Omega-6: 0.3 g, Glycemic Load: 8, Cholesterol: 0 mg, Net Carbs: 22 g. Dietary suitability: Vegan, gluten-free, low-fat. Allergen information: None.

Chickpea and Spinach Stew

INGREDIENTS

- 4 large eggs
- 1 cup fresh spinach
- 8 cherry tomatoes
- 1 tbsp olive oil
- 1 tsp dried oregano

WHY IS IT GREAT?

This Mediterranean Veggie Frittata is not just delicious but also anti-inflammatory and perfectly suited for crock pot cooking! The olive oil provides monounsaturated fats that fight inflammation, while spinach and cherry tomatoes are loaded with antioxidants like vitamin C, beta-carotene, and flavonoids to reduce oxidative stress. Oregano offers natural compounds that amplify anti-inflammatory benefits. Using a crock pot enhances these qualities by preserving nutrients through slow, gentle cooking, ensuring the ingredients retain their health-boosting properties. It's also a hands-free way to prepare the dish, making it ideal for busy lifestyles. This gluten-free, vegetarian recipe is highly versatile—easily adaptable with seasonal vegetables. Serve it as a hearty breakfast or pair with a fresh salad for a light, nourishing meal packed with vibrant flavors and health benefits!

PREPARATION

- Coat the crock pot with 1 tbsp olive oil to prevent sticking.
- In a bowl, whisk 4 large eggs with salt, pepper, and 1 tsp dried oregano.
- Place 1 cup fresh spinach into the crock pot, spreading it evenly at the base.
- Halve 8 cherry tomatoes and layer them over the spinach.
- Pour the egg mixture gently into the crock pot, ensuring the veggies are covered.
- Cover and cook on low for 2–3 hours until the frittata is set and firm.
- Garnish with fresh herbs and a lemon wedge before serving hot.

NUTRITION

Per serving: calories 220, protein 12g, total fat 16g (saturated fat 4g, monounsaturated fat 10g, polyunsaturated fat 2g), carbohydrates 6g (fiber 2g, sugars 3g, added sugars 0g), cholesterol 0mg, sodium 220mg, potassium 300mg, calcium 70mg, iron 1.5mg, magnesium 30mg, Vitamin A 600µg, Vitamin C 15mg, Vitamin D 2µg, Vitamin E 2mg, Vitamin K 120µg, Omega-3 0.1g, Omega-6 0.3g. Glycemic load is low, net carbs 4g. This gluten-free, vegetarian recipe contains no nuts or shellfish, making it suitable for most diets.

Tomato and Basil Soup

INGREDIENTS

- 1 cup chopped tomatoes
- 1 cup vegetable broth
- 2 tbsp olive oil
- 3 leaves fresh basil
- 1 clove garlic, minced

WHY IS IT GREAT?

Tomato and Basil Soup is the epitome of comforting, nutritious meals, combining simplicity with robust flavors. Fresh tomatoes and basil provide an abundance of antioxidants and anti-inflammatory properties, supporting heart health and overall wellness. Olive oil adds richness while enhancing the absorption of fat-soluble vitamins. Preparing this soup in a crock pot lets the natural sweetness of tomatoes shine as they slowly cook, creating a deep, flavorful broth. Perfect for busy days, it's an effortless way to enjoy a wholesome meal. Serve with crusty bread or a side salad for a well-rounded dish. Its bright presentation, earthy aroma, and health benefits make it a crowd-pleaser that's as visually appealing as it is satisfying. Customizable and hearty, this soup is sure to impress!

PREPARATION

- Heat 2 tbsp of olive oil in a crock pot on a sauté setting, then lightly cook 1 clove of minced garlic until fragrant.
- Add 1 cup of chopped tomatoes and stir well to coat with the garlic oil.
- Pour in 1 cup of vegetable broth, mix, and cover with the lid.
- Set the crock pot to low heat and cook for 3 hours, allowing flavors to meld.
- Blend the soup using an immersion blender until smooth, or leave chunky for texture.
- Add 3 leaves of fresh basil, stirring gently before serving.
- Garnish with additional basil and a drizzle of olive oil for enhanced flavor.

NUTRITION

Calories: 170 kcal, Protein: 2 g, Total Fat: 14 g (Saturated: 2 g, Monounsaturated: 10 g, Polyunsaturated: 2 g), Carbohydrates: 10 g (Fiber: 2 g, Sugars: 5 g, Added Sugars: 0 g), Sodium: 350 mg, Potassium: 350 mg, Calcium: 30 mg, Iron: 1.5 mg, Magnesium: 15 mg, Vitamin A: 800 IU, Vitamin C: 15 mg, Vitamin D: 0 IU, Vitamin E: 3 mg, Vitamin K: 30 µg, Vitamin B-complex: 0.2 mg, Omega-3: 0.1 g, Omega-6: 0.4 g, Glycemic Load: 5, Cholesterol: 0 mg, Net Carbs: 8 g. Dietary suitability: Vegan, gluten-free. Allergen information: None.

Butternut Squash and Ginger Soup

INGREDIENTS

- 1 cup butternut squash, diced
- 1 cup vegetable broth
- 1 tsp grated ginger
- 1 tbsp olive oil
- ½ tsp turmeric

WHY IS IT GREAT?

Butternut Squash and Ginger Soup is a comforting, nutrient-packed dish with vibrant anti-inflammatory properties. Butternut squash provides fiber and vitamin A, promoting eye and immune health, while ginger and turmeric enhance digestion and reduce inflammation. Cooking in a crock pot allows the flavors to meld beautifully over time, creating a rich and creamy texture with minimal effort. This soup is ideal for a light meal or starter, served with crusty bread or a side salad. It's easy to customize—swap turmeric for curry powder or add coconut milk for extra creaminess. Its bright orange hue, creamy consistency, and warming spices make it perfect for cozy dinners. Enjoy this sustainable, plant-based recipe for a truly wholesome dining experience!

PREPARATION

- Heat 1 tbsp of olive oil in a crock pot on a sauté setting and cook 1 tsp of grated ginger until fragrant.
- Add 1 cup of diced butternut squash and ½ tsp turmeric, stirring to coat evenly.
- Pour in 1 cup of vegetable broth, mix well, and cover with the lid.
- Set the crock pot to low heat and cook for 4 hours until the squash becomes tender.
- Blend the mixture using an immersion blender until smooth and creamy.
- Adjust seasoning with salt or pepper as needed.
- Serve hot, garnished with a drizzle of olive oil and fresh herbs for flavor.

NUTRITION

Calories: 150 kcal, Protein: 2 g, Total Fat: 9 g (Saturated: 1 g, Monounsaturated: 6 g, Polyunsaturated: 1 g), Carbohydrates: 15 g (Fiber: 3 g, Sugars: 4 g, Added Sugars: 0 g), Sodium: 300 mg, Potassium: 400 mg, Calcium: 40 mg, Iron: 1 mg, Magnesium: 25 mg, Vitamin A: 8000 IU, Vitamin C: 18 mg, Vitamin D: 0 IU, Vitamin E: 3 mg, Vitamin K: 20 µg, Vitamin B-complex: 0.3 mg, Omega-3: 0.05 g, Omega-6: 0.4 g, Glycemic Load: 6, Cholesterol: 0 mg, Net Carbs: 12 g. Dietary suitability: Vegan, gluten-free. Allergen information: None.

Tuscan White Bean Soup

INGREDIENTS

- 1 cup cooked cannellini beans
- 1 cup chopped kale
- 2 cloves garlic, minced
- 1 tbsp olive oil
- ½ tsp fresh rosemary, chopped

WHY IS IT GREAT?

Tuscan White Bean Soup is a hearty, nutritious dish brimming with Mediterranean flavors. Cannellini beans and kale provide a powerful combination of fiber, protein, and antioxidants, while rosemary and olive oil enhance its anti-inflammatory properties. The crock pot makes preparation effortless, allowing the beans to absorb the herbal aroma and garlic's sweetness. This method ensures rich, comforting flavors with minimal effort. Perfect as a standalone meal or paired with crusty bread, it's ideal for cozy dinners or meal prep. Customize with additional vegetables or spices for variety. This recipe's vibrant green kale and creamy beans create an appetizing presentation that's both satisfying and nourishing. Sustainable, simple, and wholesome, it's a must-try for mindful eating and comfort food lovers alike.

PREPARATION

- Heat 1 tbsp of olive oil in a crock pot on a sauté setting and cook 2 minced garlic cloves until fragrant.
- Add 1 cup of cooked cannellini beans and ½ tsp of fresh rosemary, stirring well to coat.
- Pour in 1 cup of water or broth and mix thoroughly.
- Set the crock pot to low heat and cook for 3 hours, allowing the flavors to meld together.
- Add 1 cup of chopped kale during the last 30 minutes of cooking, stirring occasionally.
- Season with salt and pepper to taste, and adjust consistency with additional broth if needed.
- Serve hot, garnished with fresh rosemary and a drizzle of olive oil for added richness.

NUTRITION

Calories: 180 kcal, Protein: 7 g, Total Fat: 7 g (Saturated: 1 g, Monounsaturated: 5 g, Polyunsaturated: 1 g), Carbohydrates: 22 g (Fiber: 6 g, Sugars: 1 g, Added Sugars: 0 g), Sodium: 300 mg, Potassium: 400 mg, Calcium: 50 mg, Iron: 2 mg, Magnesium: 30 mg, Vitamin A: 3000 IU, Vitamin C: 20 mg, Vitamin D: 0 IU, Vitamin E: 3 mg, Vitamin K: 120 µg, Vitamin B-complex: 0.2 mg, Omega-3: 0.1 g, Omega-6: 0.3 g, Glycemic Load: 7, Cholesterol: 0 mg, Net Carbs: 16 g. Dietary suitability: Vegan, gluten-free. Allergen information: None.

Turmeric Chicken Soup

INGREDIENTS

- 1 cup shredded chicken
- 2 cups chicken broth
- 1 cup sliced carrots
- 1 tbsp olive oil
- ½ tsp turmeric

WHY IS IT GREAT?

Turmeric Chicken Soup is a nourishing dish, perfect for boosting immunity and warming the soul. Packed with anti-inflammatory properties from turmeric and nutrients from carrots and chicken, it's both flavorful and healthful. Slow cooking in a crock pot enhances the soup's depth of flavor as the ingredients meld over hours. It's ideal for meal prep or a quick reheat for busy days. Serve with crusty bread or rice for a complete meal. Feel free to add other veggies like celery or spinach for variety. Its golden hue and vibrant aroma make it a feast for the eyes and palate. This sustainable, protein-rich recipe offers comfort, sustenance, and versatility—perfect for enjoying all year round!

PREPARATION

- Heat 1 tbsp of olive oil in a crock pot on the sauté setting and cook ½ tsp turmeric until aromatic.
- Add 1 cup of sliced carrots and sauté briefly to coat in the turmeric-infused oil.
- Stir in 1 cup of shredded chicken and mix well.
- Pour in 2 cups of chicken broth, stirring to combine.
- Set the crock pot to low heat and cook for 4 hours, allowing flavors to meld.
- Adjust seasoning with salt and pepper to taste.
- Serve hot, garnished with fresh parsley and a drizzle of olive oil for enhanced flavor.

NUTRITION

Calories: 210 kcal, Protein: 18 g, Total Fat: 10 g (Saturated: 2 g, Monounsaturated: 6 g, Polyunsaturated: 2 g), Carbohydrates: 8 g (Fiber: 2 g, Sugars: 4 g, Added Sugars: 0 g), Sodium: 400 mg, Potassium: 350 mg, Calcium: 40 mg, Iron: 1 mg, Magnesium: 20 mg, Vitamin A: 4000 IU, Vitamin C: 8 mg, Vitamin D: 5 IU, Vitamin E: 2 mg, Vitamin K: 10 µg, Vitamin B-complex: 0.5 mg, Omega-3: 0.1 g, Omega-6: 0.3 g, Glycemic Load: 3, Cholesterol: 45 mg, Net Carbs: 6 g. Dietary suitability: Gluten-free, dairy-free. Allergen information: None.

Lemon Chicken Orzo Soup

INGREDIENTS

- 1 cup shredded chicken
- 2 cups chicken broth
- ½ cup orzo pasta
- 1 tbsp olive oil
- 1 tbsp lemon juice

WHY IS IT GREAT?

Lemon Chicken Orzo Soup is a bright, hearty meal that's as comforting as it is refreshing. With tender chicken and zesty lemon, it delivers a protein-packed, immune-boosting meal. The anti-inflammatory benefits of lemon and olive oil complement the energy-sustaining orzo pasta. The crock pot preparation ensures the broth absorbs all the delicious flavors while keeping the chicken tender. Perfect for meal prep or quick reheat, this soup offers versatility—add spinach for greens or swap orzo for gluten-free pasta. Its golden hue, delicate lemon aroma, and herbal garnish make it a feast for the senses. Serve with crusty bread or crackers for a complete, wholesome dining experience. This sustainable, easy-to-make recipe is perfect for any season, offering health and flavor in every bowl!

PREPARATION

- Heat 1 tbsp of olive oil in a crock pot on the sauté setting.
- Add 1 cup of shredded chicken and stir briefly to coat in oil.
- Pour in 2 cups of chicken broth and bring to a gentle simmer.
- Stir in ½ cup of orzo pasta, ensuring even distribution.
- Set the crock pot to low heat and cook for 3 hours, stirring occasionally.
- Add 1 tbsp of lemon juice during the last 15 minutes of cooking.
- Serve hot, garnished with fresh parsley and a lemon wedge for flavor.

NUTRITION

Calories: 250 kcal, Protein: 18 g, Total Fat: 8 g (Saturated: 2 g, Monounsaturated: 5 g, Polyunsaturated: 1 g), Carbohydrates: 25 g (Fiber: 1 g, Sugars: 1 g, Added Sugars: 0 g), Sodium: 350 mg, Potassium: 300 mg, Calcium: 40 mg, Iron: 1 mg, Magnesium: 20 mg, Vitamin A: 500 IU, Vitamin C: 6 mg, Vitamin D: 5 IU, Vitamin E: 2 mg, Vitamin K: 10 µg, Vitamin B-complex: 0.5 mg, Omega-3: 0.1 g, Omega-6: 0.3 g, Glycemic Load: 9, Cholesterol: 45 mg, Net Carbs: 24 g. Dietary suitability: Contains gluten, dairy-free. Allergen information: Contains wheat.

Ratatouille Stew

INGREDIENTS

- 1 cup diced zucchini
- 1 cup diced eggplant
- 1 cup chopped bell peppers
- 1 tbsp olive oil
- ½ cup diced tomatoes

WHY IS IT GREAT?

Ratatouille Stew is a celebration of fresh vegetables and Mediterranean flavors. It's packed with antioxidants, vitamins, and minerals from zucchini, eggplant, and bell peppers, supporting heart health and reducing inflammation. Slow cooking in a crock pot ensures the vegetables retain their textures and flavors while melding into a rich and hearty stew. This dish is highly sustainable, made with seasonal produce, and adaptable to various diets. Serve it as a main course or side dish, paired with grains or bread. Add your favorite herbs to elevate its flavor profile. Its vibrant presentation and robust aroma make it as visually appealing as it is delicious. This wholesome, easy-to-make recipe is perfect for weeknight meals or entertaining guests with minimal effort!

PREPARATION

- Heat 1 tbsp of olive oil in a crock pot on a sauté setting and cook 1 cup each of diced zucchini, eggplant, and chopped bell peppers for 5 minutes.
- Add ½ cup of diced tomatoes and stir well.
- Season with salt, pepper, and optional herbs like thyme or basil for added flavor.
- Set the crock pot to low heat and cook for 3-4 hours, stirring occasionally to combine flavors.
- Check that the vegetables are tender and adjust seasoning as needed.
- Serve hot, garnished with fresh basil and a drizzle of olive oil.
- Pair with crusty bread or rice for a wholesome meal.

NUTRITION

Calories: 150 kcal, Protein: 3 g, Total Fat: 7 g (Saturated: 1 g, Monounsaturated: 5 g, Polyunsaturated: 1 g), Carbohydrates: 20 g (Fiber: 5 g, Sugars: 10 g, Added Sugars: 0 g), Sodium: 250 mg, Potassium: 400 mg, Calcium: 30 mg, Iron: 1 mg, Magnesium: 25 mg, Vitamin A: 1200 IU, Vitamin C: 70 mg, Vitamin D: 0 IU, Vitamin E: 3 mg, Vitamin K: 20 µg, Vitamin B-complex: 0.4 mg, Omega-3: 0.1 g, Omega-6: 0.3 g, Glycemic Load: 6, Cholesterol: 0 mg, Net Carbs: 15 g. Dietary suitability: Vegan, gluten-free. Allergen information: None.

Kale and Sweet Potato Soup

INGREDIENTS

- 1 cup chopped kale
- 1 cup diced sweet potatoes
- 1 tsp grated ginger
- 2 cups vegetable broth
- 1 tbsp olive oil

WHY IS IT GREAT?

Kale and Sweet Potato Soup is a hearty, nutrient-rich dish that supports a healthy lifestyle. Sweet potatoes provide energy-boosting carbohydrates and are packed with vitamin A, while kale contributes antioxidants and anti-inflammatory compounds. Ginger enhances digestion and adds a warming, spicy note. Cooking this dish in a crock pot allows flavors to develop deeply and ensures a fuss-free preparation. Perfect for cozy dinners or meal prep, this soup is highly adaptable—add lentils for protein or spices like turmeric for added health benefits. Its vibrant colors and earthy aroma make it a feast for the senses. Serve it as a standalone meal or pair it with crusty bread for a satisfying, wholesome experience. Enjoy this sustainable and delicious soup for comfort and nutrition!

PREPARATION

- Heat 1 tbsp of olive oil in the crock pot on the sauté setting and cook 1 tsp of grated ginger until fragrant.
- Add 1 cup of diced sweet potatoes and stir to coat with the ginger-infused oil.
- Pour in 2 cups of vegetable broth and mix well.
- Set the crock pot to low heat and cook for 3 hours until the sweet potatoes are tender.
- Stir in 1 cup of chopped kale during the last 30 minutes of cooking.
- Adjust seasoning with salt and pepper if needed.
- Serve warm, garnished with fresh parsley and a drizzle of olive oil.

NUTRITION

Calories: 190 kcal, Protein: 3 g, Total Fat: 8 g (Saturated: 1 g, Monounsaturated: 6 g, Polyunsaturated: 1 g), Carbohydrates: 26 g (Fiber: 4 g, Sugars: 6 g, Added Sugars: 0 g), Sodium: 300 mg, Potassium: 400 mg, Calcium: 50 mg, Iron: 1.5 mg, Magnesium: 25 mg, Vitamin A: 8000 IU, Vitamin C: 20 mg, Vitamin D: 0 IU, Vitamin E: 2 mg, Vitamin K: 120 µg, Vitamin B-complex: 0.4 mg, Omega-3: 0.1 g, Omega-6: 0.3 g, Glycemic Load: 8, Cholesterol: 0 mg, Net Carbs: 22 g. Dietary suitability: Vegan, gluten-free. Allergen information: None.

Red Pepper and Fennel Soup

INGREDIENTS

- 1 cup roasted red peppers, chopped
- ½ cup fennel, sliced
- 1 clove garlic, minced
- 1 tbsp olive oil
- 2 cups vegetable broth

WHY IS IT GREAT?

Red Pepper and Fennel Soup is a vibrant and flavorful dish that's as nutritious as it is delicious. Red peppers are rich in vitamin C and antioxidants, supporting immune health and reducing inflammation, while fennel aids digestion and brings a subtle sweetness. The crock pot is the perfect tool to draw out the natural flavors, creating a harmonious blend of ingredients with minimal effort. Customize by adding a hint of spice or a touch of cream for extra richness. Serve it as a light starter or pair it with crusty bread for a satisfying meal. The warm, bold colors and fragrant aroma make this soup a visual and sensory delight. It's a wholesome, sustainable recipe that's simple, nourishing, and perfect for any occasion!

PREPARATION

- Heat 1 tbsp of olive oil in the crock pot on the sauté setting, then cook 1 minced garlic clove until fragrant.
- Add ½ cup of sliced fennel and sauté for 2 minutes to soften slightly.
- Stir in 1 cup of roasted red peppers, coating them evenly in the aromatic oil.
- Pour in 2 cups of vegetable broth and mix thoroughly.
- Set the crock pot to low heat and cook for 3 hours, allowing the flavors to meld together.
- Blend the soup to a smooth consistency or leave chunky for texture.
- Serve warm, garnished with fresh dill and a drizzle of olive oil for added flavor.

NUTRITION

Calories: 120 kcal, Protein: 2 g, Total Fat: 7 g (Saturated: 1 g, Monounsaturated: 5 g, Polyunsaturated: 1 g), Carbohydrates: 13 g (Fiber: 3 g, Sugars: 5 g, Added Sugars: 0 g), Sodium: 300 mg, Potassium: 300 mg, Calcium: 30 mg, Iron: 1 mg, Magnesium: 20 mg, Vitamin A: 2500 IU, Vitamin C: 50 mg, Vitamin D: 0 IU, Vitamin E: 2 mg, Vitamin K: 10 µg, Vitamin B-complex: 0.3 mg, Omega-3: 0.05 g, Omega-6: 0.2 g, Glycemic Load: 4, Cholesterol: 0 mg, Net Carbs: 10 g. Dietary suitability: Vegan, gluten-free. Allergen information: None.

Seafood Cioppino

INGREDIENTS

- ½ cup shrimp, peeled and deveined
- ½ cup fish fillet, cut into chunks
- 1 cup diced tomatoes
- 1 tbsp olive oil
- 1 cup vegetable broth

WHY IS IT GREAT?

Seafood Cioppino is a delicious and nutritious dish that celebrates fresh, ocean-inspired flavors. The rich tomato base is packed with antioxidants, while the shrimp and fish provide lean protein and omega-3 fatty acids for heart and brain health. Its anti-inflammatory ingredients, like tomatoes and olive oil, make it a comforting yet wholesome meal. Cooking this dish in a crock pot allows the seafood to cook gently, ensuring tender, flaky results while letting the flavors meld beautifully. Perfect as a light dinner or an elegant appetizer, it pairs well with crusty bread or a side salad. Its vibrant colors and savory aroma make it a stunning dish to serve for any occasion, showcasing both health benefits and culinary elegance effortlessly.

PREPARATION

- Heat 1 tbsp of olive oil in the crock pot on the sauté setting and cook 1 cup of diced tomatoes for 2 minutes.
- Add ½ cup of shrimp and ½ cup of fish chunks, stirring gently to coat in the tomato mixture.
- Pour in 1 cup of vegetable broth and stir to combine.
- Season with salt, pepper, and optional herbs like thyme or parsley.
- Set the crock pot to low heat and cook for 3 hours, allowing flavors to meld.
- Stir occasionally to ensure even cooking of the seafood.
- Serve hot, garnished with fresh parsley and a drizzle of olive oil for added flavor.

NUTRITION

Calories: 180 kcal, Protein: 20 g, Total Fat: 7 g (Saturated: 1 g, Monounsaturated: 5 g, Polyunsaturated: 1 g), Carbohydrates: 8 g (Fiber: 2 g, Sugars: 4 g, Added Sugars: 0 g), Sodium: 300 mg, Potassium: 400 mg, Calcium: 40 mg, Iron: 2 mg, Magnesium: 20 mg, Vitamin A: 800 IU, Vitamin C: 12 mg, Vitamin D: 10 IU, Vitamin E: 2 mg, Vitamin K: 8 µg, Vitamin B-complex: 0.6 mg, Omega-3: 0.4 g, Omega-6: 0.1 g, Glycemic Load: 3, Cholesterol: 90 mg, Net Carbs: 6 g. Dietary suitability: Gluten-free, dairy-free. Allergen information: Contains shellfish and fish.

Eggplant and Chickpea Stew

INGREDIENTS

- 1 cup diced eggplant
- 1 cup cooked chickpeas
- 1 clove garlic, minced
- 1 tbsp olive oil
- ½ cup diced tomatoes

WHY IS IT GREAT?

Eggplant and Chickpea Stew is a wholesome, nutrient-rich dish perfect for plant-based meals. Eggplant's fiber and antioxidants, combined with protein-packed chickpeas, support digestive health and sustained energy. The tomatoes and olive oil enhance anti-inflammatory benefits while creating a hearty, satisfying flavor profile. Cooking in a crock pot allows the vegetables and chickpeas to absorb the rich tomato base, ensuring a tender and well-seasoned stew. It's a versatile dish that can be paired with rice, quinoa, or crusty bread for a complete meal. For added spice, consider including paprika or cumin. Its vibrant presentation, earthy aroma, and robust flavors make it a go-to recipe for both weeknight dinners and meal prep. Sustainable, simple, and delicious—this stew is comfort food at its finest!

PREPARATION

- Heat 1 tbsp of olive oil in the crock pot on the sauté setting, then cook 1 minced garlic clove until aromatic.
- Add 1 cup of diced eggplant and sauté for 3 minutes to soften slightly.
- Stir in 1 cup of cooked chickpeas and ½ cup of diced tomatoes, ensuring everything is well combined.
- Pour in ½ cup of water or broth, season with salt and pepper, and mix thoroughly.
- Set the crock pot to low heat and cook for 3 hours, stirring occasionally to combine flavors.
- Check for seasoning and adjust if necessary.
- Serve hot, garnished with fresh parsley and a drizzle of olive oil for added flavor.

NUTRITION

Calories: 200 kcal, Protein: 6 g, Total Fat: 8 g (Saturated: 1 g, Monounsaturated: 6 g, Polyunsaturated: 1 g), Carbohydrates: 26 g (Fiber: 7 g, Sugars: 5 g, Added Sugars: 0 g), Sodium: 300 mg, Potassium: 400 mg, Calcium: 30 mg, Iron: 2 mg, Magnesium: 30 mg, Vitamin A: 500 IU, Vitamin C: 12 mg, Vitamin D: 0 IU, Vitamin E: 2 mg, Vitamin K: 10 µg, Vitamin B-complex: 0.4 mg, Omega-3: 0.1 g, Omega-6: 0.3 g, Glycemic Load: 7, Cholesterol: 0 mg, Net Carbs: 19 g.Dietary suitability: Vegan, gluten-free. Allergen information: None.

Leek and Artichoke Soup

INGREDIENTS

- 1 cup artichoke hearts, chopped
- 1 cup sliced leeks
- 1 tbsp olive oil
- 2 cups vegetable broth
- 1 tbsp lemon juice

WHY IS IT GREAT?

Leek and Artichoke Soup is a light and refreshing recipe bursting with Mediterranean flavors. Artichokes provide fiber and antioxidants that promote digestion and reduce inflammation, while leeks offer subtle sweetness and vital nutrients. The addition of olive oil and lemon juice enhances its anti-inflammatory properties and creates a delicate balance of richness and tang. The crock pot method ensures a deeply flavorful dish with minimal effort, as the ingredients meld seamlessly over time. This soup is perfect as a light starter or paired with crusty bread for a satisfying meal. Customize it with herbs like thyme or dill for added aroma. Its vibrant, creamy presentation and healthful benefits make it a wholesome and visually appealing dish, ideal for any occasion!

PREPARATION

- Heat 1 tbsp of olive oil in the crock pot on the sauté setting and cook 1 cup of sliced leeks until fragrant.
- Add 1 cup of chopped artichoke hearts and stir gently to coat in the oil.
- Pour in 2 cups of vegetable broth and mix thoroughly.
- Set the crock pot to low heat and cook for 3 hours, allowing flavors to meld beautifully.
- Stir in 1 tbsp of lemon juice during the last 15 minutes of cooking.
- Blend the soup partially for a creamy texture or leave chunky for variety.
- Serve warm, garnished with fresh parsley and a drizzle of olive oil.

NUTRITION

Calories: 150 kcal, Protein: 3 g, Total Fat: 7 g (Saturated: 1 g, Monounsaturated: 5 g, Polyunsaturated: 1 g), Carbohydrates: 19 g (Fiber: 5 g, Sugars: 3 g, Added Sugars: 0 g), Sodium: 300 mg, Potassium: 400 mg, Calcium: 40 mg, Iron: 2 mg, Magnesium: 25 mg, Vitamin A: 500 IU, Vitamin C: 12 mg, Vitamin D: 0 IU, Vitamin E: 2 mg, Vitamin K: 10 µg, Vitamin B-complex: 0.3 mg, Omega-3: 0.05 g, Omega-6: 0.2 g, Glycemic Load: 5, Cholesterol: 0 mg, Net Carbs: 14 g. Dietary suitability: Vegan, gluten-free. Allergen information: None.

Moroccan Lentil Stew

INGREDIENTS

- ½ cup lentils
- ½ tsp ground cinnamon
- ¼ cup dried apricots, chopped
- 1 tbsp olive oil
- 1 cup vegetable broth

WHY IS IT GREAT?

Moroccan Lentil Stew is a flavorful and warming dish rich in antioxidants and nutrients. Lentils provide plant-based protein and fiber, while dried apricots add a natural sweetness and vitamin A. The hint of cinnamon enhances the anti-inflammatory benefits and infuses a unique warmth into the stew. Cooking in a crock pot ensures the flavors meld perfectly, resulting in a hearty and satisfying meal with minimal effort. It's highly versatile—add chickpeas for extra protein or fresh herbs for a refreshing twist. Serve with rice, couscous, or crusty bread to complete the dish. Its earthy, aromatic profile and beautiful presentation make it a delightful choice for cozy dinners or entertaining guests. Wholesome, sustainable, and easy to prepare, this stew is a winner!

PREPARATION

- Heat 1 tbsp of olive oil in the crock pot on the sauté setting and stir in ½ tsp of ground cinnamon until fragrant.
- Add ½ cup of lentils and ¼ cup of chopped dried apricots, mixing well.
- Pour in 1 cup of vegetable broth and stir thoroughly to combine.
- Set the crock pot to low heat and cook for 4 hours, stirring occasionally to ensure even cooking.
- Check lentils for tenderness, adjusting seasoning with salt and pepper if needed.
- Serve hot, garnished with fresh parsley and a drizzle of olive oil for a flavorful finish.
- Pair with crusty bread or rice for a complete meal.

NUTRITION

Calories: 220 kcal, Protein: 6 g, Total Fat: 7 g (Saturated: 1 g, Monounsaturated: 5 g, Polyunsaturated: 1 g), Carbohydrates: 32 g (Fiber: 8 g, Sugars: 10 g, Added Sugars: 0 g), Sodium: 300 mg, Potassium: 400 mg, Calcium: 40 mg, Iron: 2 mg, Magnesium: 30 mg, Vitamin A: 800 IU, Vitamin C: 4 mg, Vitamin D: 0 IU, Vitamin E: 2 mg, Vitamin K: 8 µg, Vitamin B-complex: 0.4 mg, Omega-3: 0.1 g, Omega-6: 0.3 g, Glycemic Load: 10, Cholesterol: 0 mg, Net Carbs: 24 g. Dietary suitability: Vegan, gluten-free. Allergen information: None.

Cauliflower Turmeric Soup

INGREDIENTS

- 1 cup cauliflower florets
- ½ tsp turmeric powder
- 1 clove garlic, minced
- 1 tbsp olive oil
- 2 cups vegetable broth

WHY IS IT GREAT?

Cauliflower Turmeric Soup is a delightful combination of creamy texture and bold flavors, offering health benefits and culinary charm. Turmeric adds anti-inflammatory properties and a warm golden hue, while cauliflower provides fiber and essential nutrients for gut health. Olive oil enhances the richness and helps absorb fat-soluble vitamins. Cooking in a crock pot ensures the flavors meld beautifully, creating a comforting and hassle-free dish. This soup is versatile—serve as a light starter or pair with crusty bread for a heartier meal. Garnish with fresh herbs or a splash of lemon juice for added zest. Its creamy texture, vibrant presentation, and wholesome ingredients make it an ideal choice for anyone seeking a simple, nutritious, and visually appealing meal.

PREPARATION

- Heat 1 tbsp of olive oil in the crock pot on the sauté setting and cook 1 minced garlic clove until fragrant.
- Add 1 cup of cauliflower florets and stir to coat with the oil.
- Sprinkle ½ tsp of turmeric powder and mix well.
- Pour in 2 cups of vegetable broth and stir thoroughly to combine.
- Set the crock pot to low heat and cook for 4 hours until the cauliflower is tender.
- Blend the soup using an immersion blender until smooth and creamy.
- Serve warm, garnished with fresh parsley and a drizzle of olive oil.

NUTRITION

Calories: 120 kcal, Protein: 3 g, Total Fat: 7 g (Saturated: 1 g, Monounsaturated: 5 g, Polyunsaturated: 1 g), Carbohydrates: 12 g (Fiber: 3 g, Sugars: 3 g, Added Sugars: 0 g), Sodium: 300 mg, Potassium: 350 mg, Calcium: 30 mg, Iron: 1 mg, Magnesium: 20 mg, Vitamin A: 300 IU, Vitamin C: 25 mg, Vitamin D: 0 IU, Vitamin E: 2 mg, Vitamin K: 8 µg, Vitamin B-complex: 0.4 mg, Omega-3: 0.05 g, Omega-6: 0.3 g, Glycemic Load: 3, Cholesterol: 0 mg, Net Carbs: 9 g. Dietary suitability: Vegan, gluten-free. Allergen information: None.

Lemon Herb Chicken

INGREDIENTS

- 2 chicken thighs
- 1 tbsp lemon juice
- 1 clove garlic, minced
- 1 tbsp olive oil
- ½ tsp dried oregano

WHY IS IT GREAT?

Lemon Herb Chicken is a simple yet flavorful dish perfect for weeknight meals or special occasions. The zesty lemon juice and aromatic oregano infuse the chicken with bright Mediterranean flavors, while garlic and olive oil enhance its richness. The dish is naturally anti-inflammatory due to the use of olive oil and oregano, promoting heart health and digestion. Cooking it in a crock pot ensures the chicken stays tender and juicy, absorbing all the savory juices over hours. This method is effortless, freeing up your time while delivering a restaurant-quality meal. Serve with a side of roasted vegetables or a fresh salad for a balanced plate. Its golden presentation and vibrant flavors make it a crowd-pleaser, offering health and indulgence in one bite!

PREPARATION

- Rub 2 chicken thighs with 1 tbsp of olive oil, 1 clove of minced garlic, and ½ tsp of dried oregano.
- Place the chicken thighs in the crock pot, ensuring even spacing.
- Squeeze 1 tbsp of lemon juice over the chicken for added flavor.
- Cover and set the crock pot to low heat, cooking for 5 hours until the chicken is tender.
- Baste occasionally with the juices to keep the chicken moist.
- Serve the chicken hot, garnished with fresh oregano and a lemon wedge for a burst of freshness.
- Pair with steamed vegetables or a side of rice for a complete meal.

NUTRITION

Calories: 250 kcal, Protein: 20 g, Total Fat: 18 g (Saturated: 3 g, Monounsaturated: 12 g, Polyunsaturated: 2 g), Carbohydrates: 1 g (Fiber: 0 g, Sugars: 0 g, Added Sugars: 0 g), Sodium: 300 mg, Potassium: 250 mg, Calcium: 20 mg, Iron: 1 mg, Magnesium: 15 mg, Vitamin A: 300 IU, Vitamin C: 6 mg, Vitamin D: 1 IU, Vitamin E: 1 mg, Vitamin K: 2 µg, Vitamin B-complex: 0.5 mg, Omega-3: 0.1 g, Omega-6: 0.4 g, Glycemic Load: 0, Cholesterol: 70 mg, Net Carbs: 1 g. Dietary suitability: Gluten-free, dairy-free. Allergen information: None.

Greek Chicken with Olives

INGREDIENTS

- 2 chicken breasts
- ¼ cup olives, halved
- 1 clove garlic, minced
- 1 tbsp olive oil
- ½ tsp dried oregano

WHY IS IT GREAT?

Greek Chicken with Olives is a flavorful and healthful dish that brings the Mediterranean to your table. The olives and olive oil provide heart-healthy monounsaturated fats and antioxidants, while oregano and garlic add anti-inflammatory properties and aromatic depth. Cooking the chicken in a crock pot ensures it stays tender and juicy, absorbing the rich, briny flavors of the olives. This dish is versatile—perfect for dinner parties or meal prep. Serve it with a side of roasted vegetables, quinoa, or pita bread for a complete meal. Its vibrant colors and savory aroma make it a visual and culinary delight. Easy to prepare, sustainably focused, and packed with wholesome ingredients, it's a dish you'll return to time and time again!

PREPARATION

- Rub 2 chicken breasts with 1 tbsp of olive oil, 1 clove of minced garlic, and ½ tsp of dried oregano.
- Place the chicken breasts in the crock pot, ensuring they lay flat.
- Add ¼ cup of halved olives evenly over the chicken.
- Cover and set the crock pot to low heat, cooking for 4 hours until the chicken is fully cooked.
- Baste the chicken occasionally with its juices for added flavor and moisture.
- Serve hot, garnished with fresh oregano and a drizzle of olive oil for a Mediterranean touch.
- Pair with a side of roasted vegetables or a fresh salad for a complete meal.

NUTRITION

Calories: 280 kcal, Protein: 26 g, Total Fat: 14 g (Saturated: 2 g, Monounsaturated: 10 g, Polyunsaturated: 1 g), Carbohydrates: 1 g (Fiber: 0 g, Sugars: 0 g, Added Sugars: 0 g), Sodium: 350 mg, Potassium: 300 mg, Calcium: 20 mg, Iron: 1 mg, Magnesium: 15 mg, Vitamin A: 200 IU, Vitamin C: 2 mg, Vitamin D: 1 IU, Vitamin E: 1 mg, Vitamin K: 3 µg, Vitamin B-complex: 0.4 mg, Omega-3: 0.1 g, Omega-6: 0.3 g, Glycemic Load: 0, Cholesterol: 70 mg, Net Carbs: 1 g. Dietary suitability: Gluten-free, dairy-free. Allergen information: None.

Turmeric and Ginger Chicken

INGREDIENTS

- 2 chicken thighs
- ½ tsp turmeric powder
- 1 tsp grated ginger
- 1 clove garlic, minced
- 1 tbsp olive oil

WHY IS IT GREAT?

Turmeric and Ginger Chicken is a flavorful, health-boosting dish perfect for any meal. Turmeric offers powerful anti-inflammatory benefits and a vibrant golden hue, while ginger supports digestion and adds a warming spiciness. The garlic and olive oil enhance both flavor and health properties, making this recipe nutrient-rich and satisfying. Cooking it in a crock pot ensures the chicken stays tender and absorbs the aromatic spices fully. This method also makes preparation stress-free, freeing up your time. Pair it with quinoa or roasted vegetables for a wholesome plate. Its warm colors and bold flavors make it as visually appealing as it is delicious. With sustainability and health in mind, this recipe is ideal for anyone seeking a simple, flavorful, and nutritious dish.

PREPARATION

- Mix 1 tbsp of olive oil, ½ tsp of turmeric powder, 1 tsp of grated ginger, and 1 clove of minced garlic.
- Coat 2 chicken thighs evenly with the spice mixture.
- Place the chicken in the crock pot, ensuring they are flat.
- Set the crock pot to low heat and cook for 5 hours, turning occasionally to ensure even cooking.
- Baste the chicken with its juices for added flavor and moisture.
- Serve warm, garnished with fresh parsley and a drizzle of olive oil.
- Pair with steamed vegetables or rice for a complete meal.

NUTRITION

Calories: 260 kcal, Protein: 22 g, Total Fat: 18 g (Saturated: 3 g, Monounsaturated: 12 g, Polyunsaturated: 2 g), Carbohydrates: 2 g (Fiber: 0 g, Sugars: 0 g, Added Sugars: 0 g), Sodium: 250 mg, Potassium: 300 mg, Calcium: 20 mg, Iron: 1 mg, Magnesium: 15 mg, Vitamin A: 200 IU, Vitamin C: 3 mg, Vitamin D: 1 IU, Vitamin E: 1 mg, Vitamin K: 2 µg, Vitamin B-complex: 0.5 mg, Omega-3: 0.1 g, Omega-6: 0.4 g, Glycemic Load: 0, Cholesterol: 70 mg, Net Carbs: 2 g. Dietary suitability: Gluten-free, dairy-free. Allergen information: None.

Moroccan Chicken

INGREDIENTS

- 2 chicken thighs
- ¼ cup dried apricots, chopped
- 2 tbsp almonds, slivered
- ½ tsp ground cinnamon
- 1 tbsp olive oil

WHY IS IT GREAT?

Moroccan Chicken is a vibrant and aromatic dish perfect for exploring bold flavors. The sweet dried apricots balance the earthy cinnamon and savory chicken, creating a harmonious blend of tastes. Almonds add a satisfying crunch and essential nutrients, while olive oil enriches the dish with healthy fats. This recipe is rich in anti-inflammatory ingredients like cinnamon and olive oil, supporting overall wellness. The crock pot ensures tender, juicy chicken infused with spices, making it an effortless yet impressive meal. Serve it with couscous or rice for a complete and satisfying dish. Its vibrant presentation and versatile flavor profile make it ideal for both weeknight dinners and special occasions. Enjoy a wholesome, flavorful, and easy-to-prepare recipe inspired by Moroccan culinary traditions!

PREPARATION

- Heat 1 tbsp of olive oil in the crock pot on the sauté setting and brown 2 chicken thighs.
- Add ¼ cup of chopped dried apricots and 2 tbsp of slivered almonds to the pot.
- Sprinkle ½ tsp of ground cinnamon evenly over the ingredients.
- Pour in ½ cup of water or broth and mix well.
- Set the crock pot to low heat and cook for 4 hours, stirring occasionally.
- Ensure the chicken is tender and well-coated in the spiced sauce.
- Serve hot, garnished with fresh parsley and a drizzle of olive oil.

NUTRITION

Calories: 320 kcal, Protein: 22 g, Total Fat: 16 g (Saturated: 3 g, Monounsaturated: 11 g, Polyunsaturated: 2 g), Carbohydrates: 18 g (Fiber: 3 g, Sugars: 10 g, Added Sugars: 0 g), Sodium: 200 mg, Potassium: 400 mg, Calcium: 40 mg, Iron: 1.5 mg, Magnesium: 30 mg, Vitamin A: 800 IU, Vitamin C: 2 mg, Vitamin D: 1 IU, Vitamin E: 2 mg, Vitamin K: 5 µg, Vitamin B-complex: 0.5 mg, Omega-3: 0.1 g, Omega-6: 0.4 g, Glycemic Load: 5, Cholesterol: 70 mg, Net Carbs: 15 g. Dietary suitability: Gluten-free, dairy-free. Allergen information: Contains nuts.

Chicken with Artichokes

INGREDIENTS

- 2 chicken thighs
- 1 cup artichoke hearts, halved
- 1 clove garlic, minced
- 1 tbsp olive oil
- ½ tsp dried thyme

WHY IS IT GREAT?

Chicken with Artichokes is a flavorful and health-conscious dish that celebrates Mediterranean ingredients. Artichokes provide fiber, antioxidants, and unique prebiotics that support gut health, while olive oil and thyme contribute anti-inflammatory benefits and robust flavor. Cooking in a crock pot ensures tender, juicy chicken infused with the rich, earthy notes of garlic and thyme. This easy-to-make dish is perfect for busy days or meal prepping. Serve with a side of roasted vegetables or rice to create a complete and satisfying meal. The vibrant presentation, with golden chicken and green artichokes, makes it as appealing as it is delicious. Its balance of taste, nutrition, and simplicity ensures it's a recipe you'll return to again and again!

PREPARATION

- Rub 2 chicken thighs with 1 tbsp of olive oil, 1 clove of minced garlic, and ½ tsp of dried thyme.
- Place the chicken thighs in the crock pot, arranging them in a single layer.
- Add 1 cup of halved artichoke hearts on top of the chicken.
- Cover and set the crock pot to low heat, cooking for 4 hours until the chicken is tender.
- Occasionally baste the chicken with its juices for enhanced flavor and moisture.
- Serve the chicken hot, garnished with fresh thyme and a drizzle of olive oil.
- Pair with quinoa or roasted potatoes for a complete meal.

NUTRITION

Calories: 240 kcal, Protein: 22 g, Total Fat: 15 g (Saturated: 3 g, Monounsaturated: 10 g, Polyunsaturated: 2 g), Carbohydrates: 4 g (Fiber: 2 g, Sugars: 1 g, Added Sugars: 0 g), Sodium: 200 mg, Potassium: 300 mg, Calcium: 30 mg, Iron: 2 mg, Magnesium: 20 mg, Vitamin A: 100 IU, Vitamin C: 4 mg, Vitamin D: 1 IU, Vitamin E: 1 mg, Vitamin K: 3 µg, Vitamin B-complex: 0.5 mg, Omega-3: 0.1 g, Omega-6: 0.3 g, Glycemic Load: 1, Cholesterol: 70 mg, Net Carbs: 2 g. Dietary suitability: Gluten-free, dairy-free. Allergen information: None.

Sweet Potato Tagine

INGREDIENTS

- 2 chicken thighs
- 1 cup sweet potato chunks
- ½ tsp ground cinnamon
- 1 tbsp olive oil
- 1 cup vegetable broth

WHY IS IT GREAT?

Sweet Potato Chicken Tagine is a delicious and healthful dish packed with flavor and nutrition. Sweet potatoes provide a natural sweetness, fiber, and vitamins, while cinnamon adds anti-inflammatory properties and warmth. The crock pot method ensures the chicken stays tender and absorbs the rich, spiced broth, creating a comforting and effortless meal. Pair it with couscous or rice for a hearty plate. Its vibrant colors and enticing aroma make it a feast for the senses. Perfect for weeknight dinners or entertaining guests, this recipe offers flexibility—add chickpeas or dried fruit for variation. The balance of savory and sweet flavors combined with a nutrient-dense profile ensures a dish that's as healthy as it is delicious. Enjoy this wholesome, easy-to-make meal!

PREPARATION

- Heat 1 tbsp of olive oil in the crock pot on the sauté setting and brown 2 chicken thighs lightly.
- Add 1 cup of sweet potato chunks and stir gently to coat with the oil.
- Sprinkle ½ tsp of ground cinnamon evenly over the chicken and sweet potatoes.
- Pour in 1 cup of vegetable broth, ensuring the ingredients are submerged.
- Set the crock pot to low heat and cook for 4 hours until the chicken is tender.
- Occasionally stir to mix flavors and ensure even cooking.
- Serve warm, garnished with fresh parsley and a drizzle of olive oil.

NUTRITION

Calories: 280 kcal, Protein: 22 g, Total Fat: 12 g (Saturated: 2 g, Monounsaturated: 8 g, Polyunsaturated: 2 g), Carbohydrates: 18 g (Fiber: 3 g, Sugars: 4 g, Added Sugars: 0 g), Sodium: 200 mg, Potassium: 400 mg, Calcium: 40 mg, Iron: 1.5 mg, Magnesium: 30 mg, Vitamin A: 6000 IU, Vitamin C: 6 mg, Vitamin D: 1 IU, Vitamin E: 1 mg, Vitamin K: 5 µg, Vitamin B-complex: 0.5 mg, Omega-3: 0.1 g, Omega-6: 0.4 g, Glycemic Load: 6, Cholesterol: 70 mg, Net Carbs: 15 g. Dietary suitability: Gluten-free, dairy-free. Allergen information: None.

Chicken with Wild Rice

INGREDIENTS

- 2 chicken thighs
- ½ cup wild rice
- ½ tsp dried rosemary
- 1 tbsp olive oil
- 1 cup chicken broth

WHY IS IT GREAT?

Chicken with Wild Rice is a wholesome and hearty dish that combines protein-packed chicken with nutrient-rich wild rice. Rosemary adds an aromatic touch, while olive oil enriches the dish with healthy fats. This recipe is naturally gluten-free and full of anti-inflammatory ingredients like olive oil and rosemary, making it a great choice for overall wellness. Cooking it in a crock pot allows the flavors to meld beautifully, ensuring tender chicken and perfectly cooked rice with minimal effort. Serve it with steamed vegetables or a fresh salad for a complete and satisfying meal. The comforting flavors, simple preparation, and visually appealing presentation make this recipe a staple for both busy weeknights and leisurely dinners. Enjoy the perfect balance of taste and nutrition!

PREPARATION

- Heat 1 tbsp of olive oil in the crock pot on the sauté setting and brown 2 chicken thighs lightly.
- Add ½ cup of wild rice, spreading evenly in the crock pot.
- Sprinkle ½ tsp of dried rosemary over the chicken and rice.
- Pour in 1 cup of chicken broth, ensuring the rice is submerged.
- Set the crock pot to low heat and cook for 4 hours until the chicken is tender and the rice is cooked.
- Stir occasionally to combine flavors evenly.
- Serve hot, garnished with fresh rosemary and a drizzle of olive oil.

NUTRITION

Calories: 290 kcal, Protein: 22 g, Total Fat: 10 g (Saturated: 2 g, Monounsaturated: 6 g, Polyunsaturated: 1 g), Carbohydrates: 20 g (Fiber: 2 g, Sugars: 1 g, Added Sugars: 0 g), Sodium: 300 mg, Potassium: 400 mg, Calcium: 30 mg, Iron: 2 mg, Magnesium: 25 mg, Vitamin A: 100 IU, Vitamin C: 2 mg, Vitamin D: 1 IU, Vitamin E: 1 mg, Vitamin K: 3 µg, Vitamin B-complex: 0.5 mg, Omega-3: 0.1 g, Omega-6: 0.3 g, Glycemic Load: 7, Cholesterol: 70 mg, Net Carbs: 18 g. Dietary suitability: Gluten-free, dairy-free. Allergen information: None.

Yogurt Dill Chicken

INGREDIENTS

- 2 chicken breasts
- ¼ cup Greek yogurt
- 1 tbsp fresh dill, chopped
- 1 clove garlic, minced
- 1 tbsp olive oil

WHY IS IT GREAT?

Yogurt Dill Chicken is a light, flavorful dish that combines creamy Greek yogurt with the refreshing taste of dill. The yogurt tenderizes the chicken while adding a tangy flavor, and dill provides a burst of freshness with anti-inflammatory benefits. Garlic and olive oil enhance the dish with aromatic richness and heart-healthy fats. The crock pot method ensures the chicken remains tender and juicy while the flavors meld beautifully. This recipe is versatile—pair it with quinoa, couscous, or a crisp green salad for a balanced meal. Its bright presentation and wholesome ingredients make it perfect for weeknight dinners or entertaining guests. Enjoy the simplicity and goodness of this Mediterranean-inspired dish, made effortlessly in a crock pot!

PREPARATION

- Mix ¼ cup of Greek yogurt, 1 tbsp of fresh dill, 1 clove of minced garlic, and 1 tbsp of olive oil in a bowl.
- Coat 2 chicken breasts evenly with the yogurt mixture and marinate for 30 minutes.
- Place the marinated chicken in the crock pot in a single layer.
- Cover and set the crock pot to low heat, cooking for 4 hours until the chicken is tender.
- Occasionally baste the chicken with its juices for added flavor.
- Serve hot, garnished with extra dill and a drizzle of olive oil.
- Pair with a side of rice or a fresh salad for a complete meal.

NUTRITION

Calories: 230 kcal, Protein: 24 g, Total Fat: 12 g (Saturated: 3 g, Monounsaturated: 7 g, Polyunsaturated: 1 g), Carbohydrates: 3 g (Fiber: 0 g, Sugars: 2 g, Added Sugars: 0 g), Sodium: 200 mg, Potassium: 300 mg, Calcium: 30 mg, Iron: 1 mg, Magnesium: 20 mg, Vitamin A: 100 IU, Vitamin C: 3 mg, Vitamin D: 1 IU, Vitamin E: 1 mg, Vitamin K: 2 µg, Vitamin B-complex: 0.4 mg, Omega-3: 0.1 g, Omega-6: 0.3 g, Glycemic Load: 1, Cholesterol: 70 mg, Net Carbs: 3 g. Dietary suitability: Gluten-free. Allergen information: Contains dairy.

Chicken Gyros Bowl

INGREDIENTS

- 2 chicken thighs, sliced
- ½ cup cucumber, sliced
- 1 clove garlic, minced
- 1 tbsp olive oil
- 1 tbsp lemon juice

WHY IS IT GREAT?

Chicken Gyros Bowl is a deliciously simple and nutritious dish inspired by Mediterranean flavors. The marinated chicken is tender and infused with garlic and lemon, while fresh cucumber adds a cooling crunch. Olive oil and lemon juice contribute healthy fats and a zesty brightness, enhancing the overall dish. Cooking the chicken in a crock pot ensures juicy results and effortless preparation. This dish is versatile—pair it with pita bread, quinoa, or a side salad for a complete meal. Packed with anti-inflammatory ingredients like olive oil and garlic, this recipe supports heart health and digestion. Its vibrant presentation and balance of flavors make it a go-to option for quick weeknight meals or casual entertaining. Enjoy wholesome Mediterranean goodness in every bite!

PREPARATION

- Mix 1 tbsp of olive oil, 1 tbsp of lemon juice, and 1 clove of minced garlic in a bowl.
- Marinate 2 sliced chicken thighs in the mixture for 30 minutes.
- Place the marinated chicken in the crock pot and cook on low heat for 4 hours.
- Occasionally stir to ensure even cooking and absorption of flavors.
- Add ½ cup of sliced cucumber to the bowl before serving.
- Drizzle the chicken with the remaining juices and garnish with fresh dill.
- Serve with a side of rice or pita bread for a wholesome meal.

NUTRITION

Calories: 240 kcal, Protein: 22 g, Total Fat: 14 g (Saturated: 2 g, Monounsaturated: 10 g, Polyunsaturated: 2 g), Carbohydrates: 3 g (Fiber: 0 g, Sugars: 1 g, Added Sugars: 0 g), Sodium: 200 mg, Potassium: 300 mg, Calcium: 20 mg, Iron: 1 mg, Magnesium: 15 mg, Vitamin A: 50 IU, Vitamin C: 5 mg, Vitamin D: 1 IU, Vitamin E: 1 mg, Vitamin K: 3 µg, Vitamin B-complex: 0.4 mg, Omega-3: 0.1 g, Omega-6: 0.3 g, Glycemic Load: 1, Cholesterol: 70 mg, Net Carbs: 3 g. Dietary suitability: Gluten-free, dairy-free. Allergen information: None.

Lemon Dill Salmon

INGREDIENTS

- 2 salmon fillets
- 1 tbsp lemon juice
- 1 clove garlic, minced
- 1 tbsp olive oil
- 1 tbsp fresh dill, chopped

WHY IS IT GREAT?

Lemon Dill Salmon is a simple yet luxurious dish bursting with fresh, vibrant flavors. The omega-3-rich salmon provides anti-inflammatory benefits, promoting heart and brain health, while dill adds a refreshing herbal note. Lemon juice and olive oil enhance the dish with zesty brightness and healthy fats. Cooking the salmon in a crock pot ensures it remains tender and moist, absorbing the garlic and dill flavors beautifully. Perfect for busy days or elegant dinners, this recipe is versatile and pairs well with a variety of sides. Serve it with a quinoa salad or steamed asparagus for a balanced meal. The ease of preparation, combined with its nutritional value and stunning presentation, makes this dish a winner for any occasion!

PREPARATION

- Mix 1 tbsp of olive oil, 1 tbsp of lemon juice, and 1 clove of minced garlic in a bowl.
- Coat 2 salmon fillets with the mixture and marinate for 15 minutes.
- Place the salmon fillets in the crock pot and sprinkle 1 tbsp of fresh dill on top.
- Set the crock pot to low heat and cook for 2 hours, checking for doneness.
- Occasionally baste the salmon with its juices for added flavor.
- Serve hot, garnished with additional fresh dill and a lemon wedge.
- Pair with steamed vegetables or rice for a complete meal.

NUTRITION

Calories: 320 kcal, Protein: 28 g, Total Fat: 20 g (Saturated: 3 g, Monounsaturated: 12 g, Polyunsaturated: 4 g), Carbohydrates: 1 g (Fiber: 0 g, Sugars: 0 g, Added Sugars: 0 g), Sodium: 150 mg, Potassium: 450 mg, Calcium: 30 mg, Iron: 1 mg, Magnesium: 25 mg, Vitamin A: 100 IU, Vitamin C: 4 mg, Vitamin D: 12 IU, Vitamin E: 1 mg, Vitamin K: 3 µg, Vitamin B-complex: 0.6 mg, Omega-3: 1.5 g, Omega-6: 0.2 g, Glycemic Load: 0, Cholesterol: 70 mg, Net Carbs: 1 g. Dietary suitability: Gluten-free, dairy-free. Allergen information: Contains fish.

Cod with Tomatoes and Olives

INGREDIENTS

- 2 cod fillets
- ½ cup diced tomatoes
- 2 tbsp sliced olives
- 1 clove garlic, minced
- 1 tbsp olive oil

WHY IS IT GREAT?

Cod with Tomatoes and Olives is a light and nutritious Mediterranean-inspired dish. The cod provides lean protein and heart-healthy omega-3s, while tomatoes add antioxidants and olives contribute healthy fats and a delightful tang. Garlic and olive oil enhance both the flavor and anti-inflammatory properties, making this dish a wholesome choice. Cooking the cod in a crock pot ensures it remains tender and flaky, fully absorbing the vibrant flavors of the toppings. Perfect for a quick and easy dinner, it pairs beautifully with a fresh salad, quinoa, or roasted vegetables. Its visually appealing presentation, combined with its health benefits and simplicity, makes this recipe a must-try for anyone looking for a delicious and nourishing meal.

PREPARATION

- Rub 2 cod fillets with 1 tbsp of olive oil and 1 clove of minced garlic.
- Place the cod fillets in the crock pot and sprinkle ½ cup of diced tomatoes over them.
- Add 2 tbsp of sliced olives, spreading evenly across the top.
- Cover the crock pot and set to low heat, cooking for 3 hours.
- Occasionally spoon the juices over the fish to enhance the flavors.
- Serve hot, garnished with fresh parsley and a lemon wedge.
- Pair with a side of roasted vegetables or rice for a complete meal.

NUTRITION

Calories: 180 kcal, Protein: 24 g, Total Fat: 7 g (Saturated: 1 g, Monounsaturated: 5 g, Polyunsaturated: 1 g), Carbohydrates: 4 g (Fiber: 1 g, Sugars: 2 g, Added Sugars: 0 g), Sodium: 300 mg, Potassium: 400 mg, Calcium: 30 mg, Iron: 1 mg, Magnesium: 20 mg, Vitamin A: 150 IU, Vitamin C: 6 mg, Vitamin D: 12 IU, Vitamin E: 1 mg, Vitamin K: 3 µg, Vitamin B-complex: 0.5 mg, Omega-3: 0.4 g, Omega-6: 0.2 g, Glycemic Load: 1, Cholesterol: 50 mg, Net Carbs: 3 g. Dietary suitability: Gluten-free, dairy-free. Allergen information: Contains fish.

Turmeric Shrimp

INGREDIENTS

- 8 oz shrimp, peeled and deveined
- ½ tsp ground turmeric
- 1 clove garlic, minced
- 1 tbsp olive oil
- 1 tbsp fresh parsley, chopped

WHY IS IT GREAT?

Turmeric Shrimp is a flavorful, health-boosting dish that's quick to prepare and packed with nutrients. Shrimp is a great source of lean protein and omega-3s, while turmeric and garlic provide anti-inflammatory and immune-supporting benefits. Olive oil adds heart-healthy fats, and fresh parsley contributes a vibrant, herbaceous finish. Cooking the shrimp in a crock pot ensures even cooking and allows the spices to fully infuse the dish. This meal is versatile—serve it as a main course or incorporate it into salads, tacos, or rice bowls. The golden color of the turmeric-coated shrimp makes for an eye-catching presentation, ensuring that it's as visually appealing as it is delicious. Perfect for a nutritious dinner with minimal effort!

PREPARATION

- Toss 8 oz of shrimp with 1 tbsp of olive oil, ½ tsp of ground turmeric, and 1 clove of minced garlic.
- Place the shrimp in the crock pot, spreading them out in a single layer.
- Cook on low heat for 2 hours, stirring halfway through to ensure even cooking.
- Just before serving, sprinkle 1 tbsp of fresh parsley over the shrimp.
- Drizzle with additional olive oil for enhanced flavor.
- Serve hot with lemon wedges and a side of steamed rice or vegetables.
- Enjoy this flavorful, vibrant dish fresh from the crock pot.

NUTRITION

Calories: 150 kcal, Protein: 18 g, Total Fat: 7 g (Saturated: 1 g, Monounsaturated: 5 g, Polyunsaturated: 1 g), Carbohydrates: 1 g (Fiber: 0 g, Sugars: 0 g, Added Sugars: 0 g), Sodium: 300 mg, Potassium: 200 mg, Calcium: 30 mg, Iron: 2 mg, Magnesium: 20 mg, Vitamin A: 100 IU, Vitamin C: 3 mg, Vitamin D: 1 IU, Vitamin E: 1 mg, Vitamin K: 5 µg, Vitamin B-complex: 0.4 mg, Omega-3: 0.5 g, Omega-6: 0.1 g, Glycemic Load: 0, Cholesterol: 90 mg, Net Carbs: 1 g. Dietary suitability: Gluten-free, dairy-free. Allergen information: Contains shellfish.

Seafood Paella

INGREDIENTS

- 8 oz shrimp, peeled and deveined
- 6 mussels, cleaned
- ½ cup diced tomatoes
- 1 tbsp olive oil
- ½ cup brown rice

WHY IS IT GREAT?

Seafood Paella is a vibrant, healthy dish that brings Mediterranean flavors to your table. Packed with lean protein from shrimp and mussels, this dish is rich in omega-3s, promoting heart and brain health. The brown rice adds fiber and a nutty flavor, while tomatoes and olive oil provide antioxidants and anti-inflammatory benefits. Cooking it in a crock pot ensures the rice absorbs all the delicious seafood flavors while the shrimp and mussels remain tender. This dish is visually stunning, with colorful ingredients and garnishes that make it perfect for both casual and elegant dinners. Its one-pot preparation minimizes cleanup and maximizes convenience, offering a flavorful, wholesome meal that's as nutritious as it is satisfying. Enjoy this Mediterranean delight!

PREPARATION

- Heat 1 tbsp of olive oil in the crock pot on sauté mode and add ½ cup of diced tomatoes.
- Stir in ½ cup of brown rice, ensuring it's coated in the tomato and oil mixture.
- Add 8 oz of shrimp and 6 mussels on top of the rice.
- Pour 1 cup of water or broth into the crock pot, covering the ingredients.
- Cook on low heat for 4 hours until the rice is tender and the seafood is cooked.
- Stir gently to combine flavors and serve hot, garnished with fresh parsley and lemon wedges.
- Pair with a crisp salad for a complete Mediterranean meal.

NUTRITION

Calories: 320 kcal, Protein: 28 g, Total Fat: 8 g (Saturated: 1 g, Monounsaturated: 5 g, Polyunsaturated: 2 g), Carbohydrates: 30 g (Fiber: 3 g, Sugars: 3 g, Added Sugars: 0 g), Sodium: 350 mg, Potassium: 400 mg, Calcium: 40 mg, Iron: 3 mg, Magnesium: 25 mg, Vitamin A: 200 IU, Vitamin C: 5 mg, Vitamin D: 15 IU, Vitamin E: 1 mg, Vitamin K: 4 µg, Vitamin B-complex: 0.6 mg, Omega-3: 0.8 g, Omega-6: 0.2 g, Glycemic Load: 8, Cholesterol: 90 mg, Net Carbs: 27 g. Dietary suitability: Gluten-free, dairy-free. Allergen information: Contains shellfish.

Saffron Mussels

INGREDIENTS

- 12 mussels, cleaned
- 1 pinch saffron threads
- 1 clove garlic, minced
- 1 tbsp olive oil
- 1 cup vegetable broth

WHY IS IT GREAT?

Saffron Mussels is a visually stunning and nutrient-rich dish, perfect for seafood lovers. Mussels are a lean source of protein and omega-3 fatty acids, promoting heart and brain health. Saffron not only adds a luxurious golden hue but also brings anti-inflammatory and antioxidant properties. The garlic and olive oil contribute to the dish's rich Mediterranean flavors while supporting overall wellness. Cooking the mussels in a crock pot allows the saffron broth to permeate each shell, creating a deeply flavorful experience. Ideal for a light yet satisfying meal, it pairs well with crusty bread or a fresh salad. The simplicity of preparation combined with its elegant presentation makes this dish suitable for any occasion, from casual dinners to festive celebrations. Enjoy a taste of the Mediterranean with every bite!

PREPARATION

- Heat 1 tbsp of olive oil in the crock pot on sauté mode and add 1 clove of minced garlic.
- Stir in 1 pinch of saffron threads to release their aroma.
- Add 1 cup of vegetable broth and bring it to a simmer.
- Place 12 cleaned mussels into the crock pot, ensuring they are partially submerged.
- Cover and cook on high for 2 hours until the mussels open.
- Stir gently to combine the saffron broth with the mussels.
- Serve hot, garnished with fresh parsley and a wedge of lemon.

NUTRITION

Calories: 150 kcal, Protein: 18 g, Total Fat: 5 g (Saturated: 1 g, Monounsaturated: 4 g, Polyunsaturated: 0.5 g), Carbohydrates: 3 g (Fiber: 0.5 g, Sugars: 0.5 g, Added Sugars: 0 g), Sodium: 450 mg, Potassium: 300 mg, Calcium: 40 mg, Iron: 3 mg, Magnesium: 20 mg, Vitamin A: 200 IU, Vitamin C: 5 mg, Vitamin D: 15 IU, Vitamin E: 1 mg, Vitamin K: 5 µg, Vitamin B-complex: 0.6 mg, Omega-3: 0.6 g, Omega-6: 0.1 g, Glycemic Load: 0, Cholesterol: 40 mg, Net Carbs: 2.5 g. Dietary suitability: Gluten-free, dairy-free. Allergen information: Contains shellfish.

Herb-Crusted Trout

INGREDIENTS

- 2 trout fillets
- 1 clove garlic, minced
- 1 tbsp fresh parsley, chopped
- 1 tbsp olive oil
- 1 tbsp lemon juice

WHY IS IT GREAT?

Herb-Crusted Trout is a flavorful, healthy dish that's easy to prepare and visually stunning. Rich in omega-3 fatty acids, trout supports heart and brain health, while parsley and garlic offer anti-inflammatory and immune-boosting properties. Olive oil enhances the flavor with healthy fats, and lemon adds a zesty brightness. Cooking the trout in a crock pot ensures even cooking and preserves its tender, flaky texture. This dish is versatile, pairing beautifully with roasted vegetables or a fresh salad. Its herbaceous crust makes it an elegant choice for both casual dinners and special occasions. The crock pot preparation minimizes effort and cleanup, allowing the flavors to meld together perfectly. Enjoy a wholesome, nutrient-packed meal with minimal hassle!

PREPARATION

- Mix 1 tbsp of olive oil, 1 clove of minced garlic, and 1 tbsp of chopped parsley in a bowl.
- Coat 2 trout fillets with the herb mixture, pressing gently to adhere.
- Place the fillets in the crock pot, ensuring they are spread out evenly.
- Drizzle with 1 tbsp of lemon juice for added flavor.
- Cook on low heat for 2.5 hours until the trout is tender and flaky.
- Garnish with additional parsley and lemon wedges before serving.
- Serve with a side of steamed vegetables or quinoa for a wholesome meal.

NUTRITION

Calories: 220 kcal, Protein: 23 g, Total Fat: 12 g (Saturated: 2 g, Monounsaturated: 8 g, Polyunsaturated: 2 g), Carbohydrates: 1 g (Fiber: 0 g, Sugars: 0 g, Added Sugars: 0 g), Sodium: 200 mg, Potassium: 400 mg, Calcium: 25 mg, Iron: 1 mg, Magnesium: 20 mg, Vitamin A: 150 IU, Vitamin C: 5 mg, Vitamin D: 20 IU, Vitamin E: 1 mg, Vitamin K: 3 µg, Vitamin B-complex: 0.6 mg, Omega-3: 1.2 g, Omega-6: 0.1 g, Glycemic Load: 0, Cholesterol: 60 mg, Net Carbs: 0.5 g. Dietary suitability: Gluten-free, dairy-free. Allergen information: Contains fish.

Tuna and Quinoa Bowl

INGREDIENTS

- 4 oz tuna, cooked or canned
- ½ cup quinoa, cooked
- 1 tbsp fresh parsley, chopped
- 1 tbsp olive oil
- 1 tbsp lemon juice

WHY IS IT GREAT?

Tuna and Quinoa Bowl is a nutritious and balanced meal, combining high-quality protein from tuna and quinoa's complete amino acids. The olive oil and lemon dressing add a fresh, zesty flavor while providing healthy fats and antioxidants. Parsley contributes a burst of freshness and anti-inflammatory benefits. Cooking in the crock pot gently warms the ingredients, allowing flavors to meld seamlessly for an elevated taste experience. This dish is perfect for a quick, satisfying lunch or dinner. It's versatile—serve it warm or chilled, and add extras like chopped vegetables or avocado for variety. Easy to prepare and full of nutrients, it's a wholesome option that's as delicious as it is healthy, ideal for busy weekdays or relaxed weekends.

PREPARATION

- Cook ½ cup of quinoa according to package instructions and set aside.
- Mix 1 tbsp of olive oil and 1 tbsp of lemon juice in a small bowl.
- Place 4 oz of cooked or canned tuna in the crock pot with the cooked quinoa.
- Drizzle the olive oil and lemon mixture over the ingredients.
- Cook on low heat for 1 hour to meld flavors and gently warm.
- Garnish with 1 tbsp of chopped parsley before serving.
- Serve hot or at room temperature, with lemon wedges for extra zest.

NUTRITION

Calories: 250 kcal, Protein: 23 g, Total Fat: 10 g (Saturated: 1.5 g, Monounsaturated: 7 g, Polyunsaturated: 1.5 g), Carbohydrates: 18 g (Fiber: 2 g, Sugars: 0.5 g, Added Sugars: 0 g), Sodium: 180 mg, Potassium: 300 mg, Calcium: 30 mg, Iron: 1.2 mg, Magnesium: 40 mg, Vitamin A: 150 IU, Vitamin C: 5 mg, Vitamin D: 10 IU, Vitamin E: 1 mg, Vitamin K: 5 µg, Vitamin B-complex: 0.8 mg, Omega-3: 0.8 g, Omega-6: 0.3 g, Glycemic Load: 3, Cholesterol: 25 mg, Net Carbs: 16 g. Dietary suitability: Gluten-free, dairy-free. Allergen information: Contains fish.

Zucchini and Fish Bake

INGREDIENTS

- 6 oz white fish fillets
- 1 medium zucchini, thinly sliced
- 1 tbsp fresh basil, chopped
- 1 tbsp olive oil
- 1 clove garlic, minced

WHY IS IT GREAT?

Zucchini and Fish Bake is a light, flavorful dish packed with nutrients. The white fish provides lean protein and omega-3 fatty acids, promoting heart and brain health. Zucchini adds a refreshing crunch with vitamins and minerals, while garlic and basil contribute anti-inflammatory and antioxidant benefits. The gentle crock pot cooking ensures the fish remains tender, and the zucchini absorbs all the infused flavors. This dish is quick to prepare, versatile, and pairs well with many sides, making it perfect for weeknight dinners or elegant gatherings. Its vibrant colors and fresh Mediterranean ingredients make it visually appealing and irresistibly delicious. Plus, minimal cleanup and nutrient retention through slow cooking make it a wholesome, effortless, and satisfying meal option.

PREPARATION

- Thinly slice 1 medium zucchini and set aside.
- In a bowl, mix 1 tbsp olive oil, 1 tbsp chopped basil, and 1 clove of minced garlic.
- Layer 6 oz white fish fillets and zucchini slices in the crock pot, alternating for even flavor distribution.
- Drizzle the olive oil mixture evenly over the fish and zucchini.
- Cook on low heat for 3 hours until the fish is flaky and the zucchini is tender.
- Garnish with fresh basil and a wedge of lemon before serving.
- Pair with a light salad or steamed rice for a complete meal.

NUTRITION

Calories: 220 kcal, Protein: 26 g, Total Fat: 10 g (Saturated: 1.5 g, Monounsaturated: 7 g, Polyunsaturated: 1 g), Carbohydrates: 5 g (Fiber: 2 g, Sugars: 2 g, Added Sugars: 0 g), Sodium: 150 mg, Potassium: 500 mg, Calcium: 40 mg, Iron: 1 mg, Magnesium: 25 mg, Vitamin A: 300 IU, Vitamin C: 10 mg, Vitamin D: 15 IU, Vitamin E: 1 mg, Vitamin K: 5 µg, Vitamin B-complex: 0.5 mg, Omega-3: 0.8 g, Omega-6: 0.2 g, Glycemic Load: 1, Cholesterol: 45 mg, Net Carbs: 3 g. Dietary suitability: Gluten-free, dairy-free. Allergen information: Contains fish.

Eggplant Parmesan

INGREDIENTS

- 1 medium eggplant, sliced
- 1 cup marinara sauce
- ¼ cup Parmesan cheese, grated
- 1 tbsp olive oil
- 1 tbsp fresh basil, chopped

WHY IS IT GREAT?

Eggplant Parmesan is a comforting, nutrient-rich dish perfect for any occasion. Packed with fiber and antioxidants from eggplant and fresh marinara, it supports digestion and combats inflammation. Parmesan cheese adds a satisfying flavor boost with calcium and protein. Using a crock pot simplifies preparation, ensuring the eggplant becomes tender and the flavors meld beautifully with minimal effort. This dish is versatile and easily adapted for dietary needs—opt for plant-based cheese for a vegan version. Its vibrant colors and Mediterranean essence make it as visually appealing as it is delicious. Serve this wholesome recipe for an effortless yet elegant meal that balances comfort and health with a delightful balance of textures and flavors.

PREPARATION

- Slice 1 medium eggplant into even rounds and set aside.
- Spread a thin layer of 1 cup marinara sauce at the bottom of the crock pot.
- Layer eggplant slices, marinara sauce, and ¼ cup grated Parmesan, repeating until all ingredients are used.
- Drizzle 1 tbsp olive oil over the top layer.
- Cook on low heat for 4 hours, allowing flavors to meld and cheese to melt.
- Garnish with 1 tbsp chopped basil before serving.
- Serve as a main dish or pair with a fresh green salad for a balanced meal.

NUTRITION

Calories: 220 kcal, Protein: 10 g, Total Fat: 12 g (Saturated: 3 g, Monounsaturated: 7 g, Polyunsaturated: 1 g), Carbohydrates: 20 g (Fiber: 7 g, Sugars: 8 g, Added Sugars: 0 g), Sodium: 400 mg, Potassium: 550 mg, Calcium: 150 mg, Iron: 1 mg, Magnesium: 25 mg, Vitamin A: 300 IU, Vitamin C: 8 mg, Vitamin D: 5 IU, Vitamin E: 1 mg, Vitamin K: 10 µg, Vitamin B-complex: 0.5 mg, Omega-3: 0.1 g, Omega-6: 0.2 g, Glycemic Load: 4, Cholesterol: 8 mg, Net Carbs: 13 g. Dietary suitability: Gluten-free (if breadcrumbs are not used), vegetarian. Allergen information: Contains dairy.

Stuffed Bell Peppers

INGREDIENTS

- 2 medium bell peppers (any color)
- ½ cup cooked quinoa
- ½ cup cooked chickpeas
- 1 clove garlic, minced
- 1 tbsp olive oil

WHY IS IT GREAT?

Stuffed Bell Peppers combine vibrant flavors with wholesome nutrition, making them a standout dish. High in fiber, antioxidants, and plant-based protein, this recipe supports gut health, boosts immunity, and reduces inflammation. The colorful peppers are rich in vitamins C and A, while quinoa and chickpeas provide essential amino acids and minerals. Slow cooking enhances flavor depth, ensures tender peppers, and keeps the meal stress-free. Easily customizable with different grains or spices, this recipe suits diverse preferences. Serve this visually stunning dish to impress guests or enjoy a simple, healthful dinner. The crock pot method locks in nutrients and requires minimal cleanup, making this meal both eco-friendly and deliciously convenient.

PREPARATION

- Cut the tops off 2 medium bell peppers and remove seeds and membranes.
- In a bowl, mix ½ cup cooked quinoa, ½ cup cooked chickpeas, 1 clove minced garlic, and 1 tbsp olive oil.
- Stuff the bell peppers with the quinoa mixture, packing it in gently.
- Place the peppers upright in the crock pot and drizzle with additional olive oil if desired.
- Cook on low heat for 4 hours until the peppers are tender.
- Garnish with fresh parsley or a squeeze of lemon before serving.
- Serve as a standalone dish or with a light salad for a complete meal.

NUTRITION

Calories: 180 kcal, Protein: 6 g, Total Fat: 6 g (Saturated: 1 g, Monounsaturated: 4 g, Polyunsaturated: 1 g), Carbohydrates: 25 g (Fiber: 6 g, Sugars: 6 g, Added Sugars: 0 g), Sodium: 100 mg, Potassium: 400 mg, Calcium: 30 mg, Iron: 1.5 mg, Magnesium: 50 mg, Vitamin A: 1,200 IU, Vitamin C: 100 mg, Vitamin D: 0 IU, Vitamin E: 1 mg, Vitamin K: 10 µg, Vitamin B-complex: 0.6 mg, Omega-3: 0.1 g, Omega-6: 0.4 g, Glycemic Load: 6, Cholesterol: 0 mg, Net Carbs: 19 g. Dietary suitability: Gluten-free, vegan. Allergen information: Contains no common allergens.

Vegetable Tagine

INGREDIENTS

- 1 cup zucchini, sliced
- 1 cup carrots, sliced
- 1 tsp turmeric
- 1 tbsp olive oil
- 1 cup vegetable broth

WHY IS IT GREAT?

Vegetable Tagine is a nutrient-packed dish full of anti-inflammatory benefits from turmeric, known to combat oxidative stress and improve joint health. The mix of zucchini and carrots provides a wealth of fiber, beta-carotene, and vitamin C. The crock pot method ensures slow, even cooking, allowing flavors to meld beautifully with minimal effort. It's versatile, pairing well with bread or grains for a complete meal, and can be customized with seasonal vegetables for added variety. With its bright, vibrant colors and warm, earthy flavor, this tagine is perfect for family meals or entertaining. Serve in a rustic dish for a homely yet elegant presentation, and enjoy the wholesome goodness of this simple and sustainable recipe!

PREPARATION

- Slice 1 cup each of zucchini and carrots and set aside.
- Heat 1 tbsp olive oil in a skillet; lightly sauté the vegetables for 2 minutes.
- Transfer vegetables to the crock pot and add 1 tsp turmeric.
- Pour in 1 cup vegetable broth to ensure a rich base.
- Cover and cook on low heat for 4 hours until the vegetables are tender.
- Garnish with fresh herbs like parsley before serving.
- Serve warm with crusty bread or couscous for a hearty meal.

NUTRITION

Calories: 120 kcal, Protein: 2 g, Total Fat: 5 g (Saturated: 0.5 g, Monounsaturated: 3.5 g, Polyunsaturated: 0.5 g), Carbohydrates: 15 g (Fiber: 3 g, Sugars: 6 g, Added Sugars: 0 g), Sodium: 400 mg, Potassium: 400 mg, Calcium: 30 mg, Iron: 1 mg, Magnesium: 20 mg, Vitamin A: 8000 IU, Vitamin C: 12 mg, Vitamin D: 0 IU, Vitamin E: 1 mg, Vitamin K: 5 µg, Vitamin B-complex: 0.3 mg, Omega-3: 0 g, Omega-6: 0.2 g, Glycemic Load: 5, Cholesterol: 0 mg, Net Carbs: 12 g. Dietary suitability: Vegan, gluten-free. Allergen information: None.

Sweet Potato Curry

INGREDIENTS

- 2 cups sweet potatoes, cubed
- 1 cup chickpeas, cooked
- 1 cup coconut milk
- 1 tsp turmeric
- 2 cloves garlic, minced

WHY IS IT GREAT?

Sweet Potato Curry is a delightful fusion of creamy and hearty flavors, with turmeric offering anti-inflammatory properties. Sweet potatoes provide a rich source of beta-carotene and fiber, while chickpeas add protein for a balanced meal. The coconut milk enhances the dish with healthy fats, making it both satisfying and nourishing. Cooking in a crock pot allows the spices to infuse deeply into the ingredients, creating a dish that's both aromatic and flavorful. Perfect for meal prepping or family dinners, this curry pairs beautifully with rice or flatbread. Garnish with fresh herbs for a vibrant presentation, and feel free to add seasonal vegetables for variety. It's sustainable, wholesome, and easy to adapt for diverse palates, ensuring it's always a crowd-pleaser!

PREPARATION

- Peel and cube 2 cups of sweet potatoes; mince 2 garlic cloves.
- Add sweet potatoes, chickpeas, turmeric, and minced garlic to the crock pot.
- Pour in 1 cup coconut milk, ensuring all ingredients are evenly coated.
- Stir ingredients gently to combine the flavors and prevent sticking.
- Cover and cook on low heat for 4-6 hours until sweet potatoes are tender.
- Stir halfway through cooking to maintain consistency.
- Serve hot with fresh cilantro garnish and a side of naan or rice for a wholesome meal.

NUTRITION

Calories: 280 kcal, Protein: 6 g, Total Fat: 14 g (Saturated: 12 g, Monounsaturated: 1 g, Polyunsaturated: 0.5 g), Carbohydrates: 34 g (Fiber: 6 g, Sugars: 8 g, Added Sugars: 0 g), Sodium: 320 mg, Potassium: 600 mg, Calcium: 50 mg, Iron: 2 mg, Magnesium: 40 mg, Vitamin A: 12000 IU, Vitamin C: 10 mg, Vitamin D: 0 IU, Vitamin E: 1 mg, Vitamin K: 5 µg, Vitamin B-complex: 0.3 mg, Omega-3: 0 g, Omega-6: 0.2 g, Glycemic Load: 12, Cholesterol: 0 mg, Net Carbs: 28 g. Dietary suitability: Vegan, gluten-free. Allergen information: Contains coconut.

Cauliflower Masala

INGREDIENTS

- 2 cups cauliflower florets
- 1 tsp turmeric
- 1 cup coconut milk
- 2 cloves garlic
- 1 tbsp olive oil

WHY IS IT GREAT?

Cauliflower Masala is a delightful fusion of nutrition and flavor! Turmeric is a potent anti-inflammatory and antioxidant, making this dish a fantastic choice for supporting joint health and boosting immunity. Coconut milk adds a creamy texture while keeping it dairy-free. The crock pot method ensures deep flavor development and makes it incredibly easy—just toss in the ingredients and let it cook! Serve this aromatic dish as a main course or side, and pair it with rice or flatbread. The vibrant color and rich taste make it an eye-catching and satisfying meal for any occasion. Don't hesitate to try variations like adding chickpeas or fresh spinach for extra nutrients and texture!

PREPARATION

- Wash cauliflower and cut it into bite-sized florets.
- Finely mince garlic and sauté in olive oil for 1 minute.
- Place cauliflower, garlic, turmeric, and coconut milk in the crock pot. Stir to mix evenly.
- Add 1/2 cup water and stir gently.
- Set the crock pot on low heat and cook for 5 hours until the cauliflower is tender.
- In the last 30 minutes, stir thoroughly to ensure even flavor distribution.
- Serve warm, garnished with fresh herbs and a squeeze of lemon.

NUTRITION

Calories, 200; Protein, 3g; Total Fat, 14g; Saturated Fat, 12g; Monounsaturated Fat, 1g; Polyunsaturated Fat, 1g; Carbohydrates, 15g; Fiber, 5g; Sugars, 4g; Added Sugars, 0g; Net Carbs, 10g; Sodium, 200mg; Potassium, 500mg; Calcium, 40mg; Iron, 2.5mg; Magnesium, 30mg; Vitamin A, 100 IU; Vitamin C, 50mg; Vitamin D, 0 IU; Vitamin E, 1mg; Vitamin K, 20mcg; Omega-3, 0.05g; Omega-6, 0.2g; Cholesterol, 0mg. Dietary Suitability: gluten-free, vegan. Allergen Information: none.

White Bean Ragout

INGREDIENTS

- 1 cup cannellini beans
- 1 cup diced tomatoes
- 2 cloves garlic
- 1 tbsp olive oil
- 2 tbsp chopped parsley

WHY IS IT GREAT?

White Bean Ragout is the ultimate comfort food with a healthy twist! Cannellini beans are protein-packed and fiber-rich, while tomatoes and garlic offer anti-inflammatory and heart-healthy benefits. The crock pot method enhances the flavors of this Mediterranean dish effortlessly, making it tender and savory without constant attention. It's perfect for busy days or cozy meals. This recipe is highly versatile—swap parsley with basil or add spinach for extra nutrients. The slow-cooked texture and aromatic appeal make it an irresistible meal. Pair with crusty bread or serve over rice for a complete dish. It's sustainable, plant-based, and packed with nutrients to fuel your day while being kind to the planet. You'll love how easy and satisfying it is!

PREPARATION

- Rinse cannellini beans thoroughly if using canned; if dried, soak overnight.
- Finely chop garlic and sauté in olive oil for 1 minute.
- Add beans, diced tomatoes, garlic, and 1/2 cup water or vegetable stock to the crock pot.
- Stir gently to combine ingredients evenly.
- Set the crock pot to low heat and cook for 5 hours, stirring occasionally.
- Add parsley in the final 15 minutes for maximum freshness and flavor.
- Serve hot, drizzled with olive oil and garnished with additional parsley.

NUTRITION

Calories, 220; Protein, 9g; Total Fat, 7g; Saturated Fat, 1g; Monounsaturated Fat, 5g; Polyunsaturated Fat, 1g; Carbohydrates, 30g; Fiber, 9g; Sugars, 5g; Added Sugars, 0g; Net Carbs, 21g; Sodium, 300mg; Potassium, 700mg; Calcium, 60mg; Iron, 2.5mg; Magnesium, 50mg; Vitamin A, 500 IU; Vitamin C, 15mg; Vitamin D, 0 IU; Vitamin E, 2mg; Vitamin K, 40mcg; Omega-3, 0.1g; Omega-6, 0.2g; Cholesterol, 0mg. Dietary Suitability: gluten-free, vegan. Allergen Information: none.

Ratatouille Quinoa Bake

INGREDIENTS

- 1 cup cooked quinoa
- 1 cup diced zucchini
- 1 cup diced eggplant
- 1 cup diced tomatoes
- 1 tbsp olive oil

WHY IS IT GREAT?

Ratatouille Quinoa Bake is a wholesome, nutrient-packed dish with a delicious blend of flavors! Quinoa provides a complete source of protein, while zucchini, eggplant, and tomatoes contribute antioxidants and anti-inflammatory benefits. Olive oil adds healthy fats that enhance the dish's richness. Cooking in a crock pot is a time-saver and ensures the ingredients meld together beautifully, creating a tender, flavorful bake. It's versatile—add fresh herbs or substitute squash for zucchini to customize. This recipe is eco-friendly, packed with plant-based ingredients, and perfect for any meal. Serve it as a main dish or a hearty side. The rustic presentation makes it visually appealing, and the minimal effort required makes it a must-try for busy yet health-conscious individuals!

PREPARATION

- Cook quinoa according to package instructions and set aside.
- Dice zucchini, eggplant, and tomatoes into uniform pieces for even cooking.
- Sauté zucchini and eggplant in olive oil for 2 minutes to enhance their flavor.
- Layer cooked quinoa, sautéed vegetables, and tomatoes in the crock pot.
- Stir gently, add 1/4 cup water, and cook on low heat for 3 hours.
- Mix well before serving to distribute flavors evenly.
- Garnish with fresh herbs and serve hot, drizzled with olive oil.

NUTRITION

Calories, 250; Protein, 8g; Total Fat, 7g; Saturated Fat, 1g; Monounsaturated Fat, 5g; Polyunsaturated Fat, 1g; Carbohydrates, 40g; Fiber, 8g; Sugars, 6g; Added Sugars, 0g; Net Carbs, 32g; Sodium, 200mg; Potassium, 700mg; Calcium, 40mg; Iron, 2mg; Magnesium, 60mg; Vitamin A, 700 IU; Vitamin C, 20mg; Vitamin D, 0 IU; Vitamin E, 2mg; Vitamin K, 25mcg; Omega-3, 0.1g; Omega-6, 0.2g; Cholesterol, 0mg. Dietary Suitability: gluten-free, vegan. Allergen Information: none.

Coconut Chickpeas

INGREDIENTS

- 1 cup chickpeas
- 1 cup coconut milk
- 1 tsp turmeric
- 2 cloves garlic
- 2 tbsp chopped parsley

WHY IS IT GREAT?

Coconut Chickpeas are a creamy, comforting, and nutritious delight! The combination of turmeric, coconut milk, and chickpeas offers anti-inflammatory and immune-boosting benefits, making it ideal for maintaining good health. Cooking this dish in a crock pot enhances the flavors as the spices infuse the chickpeas slowly, creating a rich and satisfying meal with minimal effort. Perfect for busy days! Add greens like spinach for extra nutrients or adjust the spice level to your liking. This dish is eco-friendly and plant-based, aligning with sustainable eating practices. Serve it with rice, quinoa, or flatbread for a complete and delicious meal. The vibrant color and creamy texture make it a showstopper on any table while being incredibly easy to prepare!

PREPARATION

- Rinse chickpeas if using canned or soak dried ones overnight.
- Mince garlic finely to release its flavor.
- Add chickpeas, coconut milk, garlic, turmeric, and 1/4 cup water to the crock pot.
- Stir ingredients gently to combine evenly.
- Set the crock pot on low heat and cook for 4 hours, stirring occasionally.
- Add parsley during the last 15 minutes to retain freshness and flavor.
- Serve warm, drizzled with additional coconut milk and garnished with parsley.

NUTRITION

Calories, 300; Protein, 9g; Total Fat, 18g; Saturated Fat, 15g; Monounsaturated Fat, 1g; Polyunsaturated Fat, 0.5g; Carbohydrates, 28g; Fiber, 7g; Sugars, 4g; Added Sugars, 0g; Net Carbs, 21g; Sodium, 200mg; Potassium, 650mg; Calcium, 50mg; Iron, 3.5mg; Magnesium, 50mg; Vitamin A, 100 IU; Vitamin C, 10mg; Vitamin D, 0 IU; Vitamin E, 0.5mg; Vitamin K, 25mcg; Omega-3, 0.05g; Omega-6, 0.2g; Cholesterol, 0mg. Dietary Suitability: gluten-free, vegan. Allergen Information: contains coconut.

Mushroom Stroganoff

INGREDIENTS

- 2 cups sliced mushrooms
- 1/2 cup cashew cream
- 2 cloves garlic
- 1 tbsp olive oil
- 1 tsp thyme

WHY IS IT GREAT?

Mushroom Stroganoff is a creamy, savory dish that's packed with flavor and health benefits! The mushrooms provide immune-boosting nutrients and a meaty texture, while the cashew cream adds a velvety richness without dairy. Thyme and garlic enhance its anti-inflammatory and antioxidant properties, making it a great choice for overall health. Slow-cooking in a crock pot allows the flavors to meld beautifully while requiring minimal effort—just set it and forget it! Serve it over pasta, rice, or mashed potatoes for a versatile, satisfying meal. The recipe is eco-friendly and fully plant-based, perfect for sustainable and conscious eating. Customize it by adding spinach or substituting cashew cream with almond cream. It's a comfort food classic reimagined for a modern, health-focused lifestyle!

PREPARATION

- Clean and slice mushrooms thinly for even cooking.
- Mince garlic finely to release its aromatic flavors.
- Add mushrooms, garlic, cashew cream, thyme, and olive oil to the crock pot.
- Stir gently to combine ingredients evenly.
- Cook on low heat for 4 hours, stirring occasionally for consistency.
- Adjust seasoning if needed and stir in extra thyme for garnish.
- Serve warm, drizzled with additional cashew cream and a sprinkle of thyme.

NUTRITION

Calories, 250; Protein, 8g; Total Fat, 16g; Saturated Fat, 3g; Monounsaturated Fat, 10g; Polyunsaturated Fat, 3g; Carbohydrates, 20g; Fiber, 3g; Sugars, 2g; Added Sugars, 0g; Net Carbs, 17g; Sodium, 150mg; Potassium, 650mg; Calcium, 40mg; Iron, 3mg; Magnesium, 50mg; Vitamin A, 100 IU; Vitamin C, 2mg; Vitamin D, 2 IU; Vitamin E, 1mg; Vitamin K, 10mcg; Omega-3, 0.1g; Omega-6, 0.3g; Cholesterol, 0mg. Dietary Suitability: gluten-free, vegan. Allergen Information: contains cashews.

Lemon Herb Farro

INGREDIENTS

- 1 cup cooked farro
- 2 tbsp chopped parsley
- 1 tbsp lemon juice
- 1 tbsp olive oil
- 2 cloves garlic

WHY IS IT GREAT?

Lemon Herb Farro is a refreshing and hearty dish, packed with whole-grain goodness and bright Mediterranean flavors! Farro is a fiber-rich ancient grain that supports digestive health, while parsley and garlic offer anti-inflammatory and antioxidant benefits. Lemon juice adds a zesty touch and boosts vitamin C intake. Cooking this recipe in a crock pot ensures perfectly tender farro with minimal effort, making it ideal for busy schedules. Serve it as a side dish or pair it with roasted vegetables for a complete meal. The slow-cooked flavors meld beautifully, creating a dish that's both simple and satisfying. Add your favorite herbs or vegetables for variety. It's a sustainable, plant-based recipe that's sure to become a go-to in your kitchen!

PREPARATION

- Rinse farro under cold water and soak for 15 minutes.
- Mince garlic finely for maximum flavor release.
- Add farro, garlic, 2 cups water, and olive oil to the crock pot.
- Cook on low heat for 4 hours or until the farro is tender and water is absorbed.
- Mix in lemon juice and parsley during the last 15 minutes of cooking.
- Stir thoroughly to combine flavors and adjust seasoning if needed.
- Serve warm, garnished with extra parsley and a drizzle of olive oil.

NUTRITION

Calories, 250; Protein, 7g; Total Fat, 7g; Saturated Fat, 1g; Monounsaturated Fat, 5g; Polyunsaturated Fat, 1g; Carbohydrates, 40g; Fiber, 6g; Sugars, 2g; Added Sugars, 0g; Net Carbs, 34g; Sodium, 100mg; Potassium, 300mg; Calcium, 20mg; Iron, 2mg; Magnesium, 70mg; Vitamin A, 200 IU; Vitamin C, 10mg; Vitamin D, 0 IU; Vitamin E, 1mg; Vitamin K, 20mcg; Omega-3, 0.05g; Omega-6, 0.1g; Cholesterol, 0mg. Dietary Suitability: vegetarian, dairy-free. Allergen Information: contains gluten (from farro).

Couscous with Olives

INGREDIENTS

- 1 cup cooked whole-grain couscous
- 1/4 cup sliced olives
- 1 tbsp olive oil
- 2 tbsp chopped sun-dried tomatoes
- 1 tsp oregano

WHY IS IT GREAT?

Couscous with Olives is a quick and delightful Mediterranean dish that's full of flavor and nutrients! The whole-grain couscous provides energy and fiber, while olives and olive oil add healthy fats and antioxidants. Sun-dried tomatoes bring a tangy depth, and oregano enhances its anti-inflammatory properties. This dish is perfect for busy days and light meals. Cooking in a crock pot allows the flavors to meld together beautifully while keeping it simple. Pair it with grilled vegetables or a side salad for a complete meal. The recipe is sustainable, as it uses plant-based ingredients with a low environmental impact. You can customize it by adding fresh herbs or substituting whole-grain quinoa for couscous. It's a vibrant, healthy, and versatile addition to any menu!

PREPARATION

- Prepare couscous according to package instructions and set aside.
- Slice olives thinly and chop sun-dried tomatoes into small pieces.
- Add cooked couscous, olives, sun-dried tomatoes, olive oil, and oregano to the crock pot.
- Stir ingredients thoroughly to combine flavors evenly.
- Set the crock pot on low heat and warm the mixture for 1 hour.
- Stir once more before serving to ensure even heat distribution.
- Serve hot, garnished with additional oregano and a drizzle of olive oil.

NUTRITION

Calories, 250; Protein, 6g; Total Fat, 10g; Saturated Fat, 1.5g; Monounsaturated Fat, 7g; Polyunsaturated Fat, 1g; Carbohydrates, 34g; Fiber, 4g; Sugars, 2g; Added Sugars, 0g; Net Carbs, 30g; Sodium, 250mg; Potassium, 300mg; Calcium, 40mg; Iron, 1.5mg; Magnesium, 30mg; Vitamin A, 50 IU; Vitamin C, 5mg; Vitamin D, 0 IU; Vitamin E, 1mg; Vitamin K, 15mcg; Omega-3, 0.05g; Omega-6, 0.2g; Cholesterol, 0mg. Dietary Suitability: vegetarian, dairy-free. Allergen Information: contains gluten (from couscous).

Turmeric Cauliflower Rice

INGREDIENTS

- 2 cups grated cauliflower
- 1 tsp turmeric
- 2 cloves garlic
- 1 tbsp olive oil
- 2 tbsp chopped parsley

WHY IS IT GREAT?

Turmeric Cauliflower Rice is a vibrant, healthy, and anti-inflammatory dish! Cauliflower provides a low-carb base rich in fiber and antioxidants, while turmeric's curcumin content supports joint health and reduces inflammation. Olive oil and garlic enhance its Mediterranean flair and contribute heart-healthy benefits. Cooking it in a crock pot is simple and fuss-free, allowing the spices to infuse deeply into the cauliflower while retaining its texture. This dish is versatile—serve it as a side for grilled vegetables, as a base for curries, or add chickpeas for extra protein. The bright golden hue makes it visually appealing, and it's customizable with herbs or spices to suit your taste. Perfect for busy days, this sustainable, plant-based recipe is both delicious and nourishing!

PREPARATION

- Grate the cauliflower into rice-sized pieces using a food processor or grater.
- Mince garlic finely for enhanced flavor.
- Add cauliflower, turmeric, garlic, and olive oil to the crock pot.
- Stir to combine all ingredients evenly, ensuring the turmeric coats the cauliflower.
- Cook on low heat for 2 hours, stirring occasionally to prevent sticking.
- Add parsley during the last 10 minutes for freshness and vibrant color.
- Serve warm, garnished with additional parsley and a drizzle of olive oil.

NUTRITION

Calories, 120; Protein, 2g; Total Fat, 7g; Saturated Fat, 1g; Monounsaturated Fat, 5g; Polyunsaturated Fat, 1g; Carbohydrates, 11g; Fiber, 4g; Sugars, 3g; Added Sugars, 0g; Net Carbs, 7g; Sodium, 80mg; Potassium, 400mg; Calcium, 30mg; Iron, 1mg; Magnesium, 20mg; Vitamin A, 200 IU; Vitamin C, 50mg; Vitamin D, 0 IU; Vitamin E, 1mg; Vitamin K, 15mcg; Omega-3, 0.05g; Omega-6, 0.1g; Cholesterol, 0mg. Dietary Suitability: gluten-free, vegan. Allergen Information: none.

Garlic Roasted Potatoes

INGREDIENTS

- 2 cups diced potatoes
- 2 cloves garlic
- 1 tbsp olive oil
- 1 tsp chopped rosemary
- 1/2 tsp black pepper

WHY IS IT GREAT?

Garlic Roasted Potatoes are a versatile and comforting dish, packed with flavor and simple ingredients! Potatoes provide a hearty base rich in potassium and vitamin C, while garlic and rosemary offer anti-inflammatory and antioxidant benefits. Olive oil contributes heart-healthy fats, making this a balanced side dish or main course. The crock pot method ensures the potatoes cook evenly, becoming tender and infused with aromatic flavors. It's a hands-off, energy-efficient way to achieve roasted perfection. Serve these potatoes alongside grilled vegetables, salads, or protein dishes for a complete meal. You can customize the recipe with your favorite herbs or spices, like thyme or smoked paprika. These golden, crispy delights are a must-try for any occasion!

PREPARATION

- Wash and dice potatoes into evenly sized cubes for uniform cooking.
- Mince garlic finely to maximize flavor.
- Add potatoes, garlic, olive oil, rosemary, and black pepper to the crock pot.
- Stir ingredients to coat the potatoes evenly with oil and seasoning.
- Cook on high heat for 3 hours, stirring occasionally to prevent sticking.
- Check for doneness and adjust seasoning if necessary in the last 30 minutes.
- Serve hot, garnished with additional rosemary and a drizzle of olive oil.

NUTRITION

Calories, 180; Protein, 3g; Total Fat, 6g; Saturated Fat, 1g; Monounsaturated Fat, 4g; Polyunsaturated Fat, 1g; Carbohydrates, 28g; Fiber, 3g; Sugars, 1g; Added Sugars, 0g; Net Carbs, 25g; Sodium, 50mg; Potassium, 600mg; Calcium, 20mg; Iron, 1.5mg; Magnesium, 30mg; Vitamin A, 5 IU; Vitamin C, 10mg; Vitamin D, 0 IU; Vitamin E, 1mg; Vitamin K, 5mcg; Omega-3, 0.05g; Omega-6, 0.1g; Cholesterol, 0mg. Dietary Suitability: gluten-free, vegan. Allergen Information: none.

Vegetable Ratatouille

INGREDIENTS

- 1 cup diced zucchini
- 1 cup diced eggplant
- 1 cup diced bell peppers
- 1 tbsp olive oil
- 1 cup diced tomatoes

WHY IS IT GREAT?

Vegetable Ratatouille is a colorful, nutrient-packed dish that celebrates the best of Mediterranean flavors! The blend of zucchini, eggplant, bell peppers, and tomatoes creates a vibrant medley rich in vitamins and antioxidants. Olive oil adds heart-healthy fats, while the slow cooking process enhances the natural sweetness and aroma of the vegetables. The recipe is perfect for the crock pot, allowing the ingredients to meld into a comforting, flavorful dish with minimal effort. It's a versatile dish—serve it as a main course, a side dish, or even a topping for grains or pasta. Customize with herbs like thyme or basil for added flavor. This sustainable, plant-based recipe is as visually appealing as it is delicious and healthy!

PREPARATION

- Dice zucchini, eggplant, bell peppers, and tomatoes into uniform pieces for even cooking.
- Add all diced vegetables to the crock pot along with olive oil and stir to coat evenly.
- Season with salt and pepper if desired, then mix gently.
- Cook on low heat for 5 hours, stirring occasionally to ensure even cooking.
- Check vegetables for tenderness and adjust seasoning during the last 30 minutes.
- Serve warm, garnished with fresh herbs and a drizzle of olive oil.

NUTRITION

Calories, 150; Protein, 3g; Total Fat, 7g; Saturated Fat, 1g; Monounsaturated Fat, 5g; Polyunsaturated Fat, 1g; Carbohydrates, 20g; Fiber, 6g; Sugars, 8g; Added Sugars, 0g; Net Carbs, 14g; Sodium, 200mg; Potassium, 600mg; Calcium, 40mg; Iron, 2mg; Magnesium, 30mg; Vitamin A, 500 IU; Vitamin C, 60mg; Vitamin D, 0 IU; Vitamin E, 2mg; Vitamin K, 25mcg; Omega-3, 0.05g; Omega-6, 0.2g; Cholesterol, 0mg. Dietary Suitability: gluten-free, vegan. Allergen Information: none.

Spiced Lentils

INGREDIENTS

- 1 cup lentils
- 1 tsp cumin
- 2 cloves garlic
- 1 tbsp olive oil
- 2 tbsp chopped parsley

WHY IS IT GREAT?

Spiced Lentils is a warming, protein-packed dish that's simple to prepare and full of flavor! Lentils are rich in fiber, plant-based protein, and iron, making them a nutritional powerhouse. Cumin and garlic add earthy, anti-inflammatory benefits while olive oil contributes heart-healthy fats. Cooking this dish in a crock pot allows the spices to deeply infuse the lentils, creating a savory, aromatic meal with minimal effort. Serve it with rice, flatbread, or a fresh salad for a complete, satisfying meal. Customize with your favorite herbs or add vegetables like spinach or carrots for extra nutrients. This dish is sustainable, plant-based, and budget-friendly, making it perfect for anyone seeking delicious, healthy, and environmentally conscious meals. You'll love how easy and versatile it is!

PREPARATION

- Rinse lentils thoroughly under cold water to remove any impurities.
- Mince garlic finely to enhance its flavor in the dish.
- Add lentils, cumin, garlic, and 2 cups of water or vegetable stock to the crock pot.
- Drizzle olive oil over the ingredients and stir gently to combine.
- Set the crock pot on low heat and cook for 5 hours, stirring occasionally.
- Stir in parsley during the last 15 minutes for a fresh, herby finish.
- Serve warm, garnished with additional parsley and a drizzle of olive oil.

NUTRITION

Calories, 250; Protein, 13g; Total Fat, 7g; Saturated Fat, 1g; Monounsaturated Fat, 5g; Polyunsaturated Fat, 1g; Carbohydrates, 30g; Fiber, 12g; Sugars, 2g; Added Sugars, 0g; Net Carbs, 18g; Sodium, 150mg; Potassium, 600mg; Calcium, 50mg; Iron, 3.5mg; Magnesium, 50mg; Vitamin A, 150 IU; Vitamin C, 10mg; Vitamin D, 0 IU; Vitamin E, 1mg; Vitamin K, 20mcg; Omega-3, 0.1g; Omega-6, 0.2g; Cholesterol, 0mg. Dietary Suitability: gluten-free, vegan. Allergen Information: none.

Greek Green Beans

INGREDIENTS

- 2 cups green beans
- 1 cup diced tomatoes
- 2 cloves garlic
- 1 tbsp olive oil
- 1 tsp oregano

WHY IS IT GREAT?

Greek Green Beans is a light, flavorful dish rich in nutrients and anti-inflammatory properties! Green beans provide a healthy dose of fiber, while tomatoes offer antioxidants like lycopene. Garlic and oregano bring Mediterranean zest and support immune health, complemented by heart-healthy olive oil. The crock pot method slowly melds the flavors, ensuring tender green beans and a deeply savory sauce with minimal effort. It's a versatile dish—serve it as a side or pair it with grains or crusty bread for a complete meal. Customizable and plant-based, it's an eco-friendly recipe perfect for any occasion. The bright colors and delicious aromas make it a joy to prepare and enjoy. You'll love how easy it is to bring authentic Mediterranean flavors to your table!

PREPARATION

- Wash and trim green beans, cutting them into uniform lengths for even cooking.
- Mince garlic finely to enhance the dish's flavor.
- Add green beans, tomatoes, garlic, and olive oil to the crock pot.
- Sprinkle oregano over the ingredients and stir gently to combine.
- Cook on low heat for 4 hours, stirring occasionally for even cooking.
- Taste and adjust seasoning during the last 30 minutes if needed.
- Serve warm, garnished with additional oregano and a drizzle of olive oil.

NUTRITION

Calories, 120; Protein, 3g; Total Fat, 7g; Saturated Fat, 1g; Monounsaturated Fat, 5g; Polyunsaturated Fat, 1g; Carbohydrates, 13g; Fiber, 4g; Sugars, 6g; Added Sugars, 0g; Net Carbs, 9g; Sodium, 200mg; Potassium, 400mg; Calcium, 40mg; Iron, 1.5mg; Magnesium, 25mg; Vitamin A, 800 IU; Vitamin C, 20mg; Vitamin D, 0 IU; Vitamin E, 1mg; Vitamin K, 15mcg; Omega-3, 0.05g; Omega-6, 0.1g; Cholesterol, 0mg. Dietary Suitability: gluten-free, vegan. Allergen Information: none.

Wild Rice Pilaf

INGREDIENTS

- 1 cup cooked wild rice
- 1 tsp orange zest
- 1 tbsp olive oil
- 1 tsp thyme
- 2 cloves garlic

WHY IS IT GREAT?

Wild Rice Pilaf is a fragrant and hearty dish that's both nutritious and delicious! Wild rice is rich in fiber and protein, supporting digestion and energy levels. Orange zest and thyme add a refreshing, anti-inflammatory boost, while garlic and olive oil bring heart-healthy benefits. The crock pot method allows the flavors to meld perfectly while keeping the preparation effortless. This versatile dish can be served as a side to complement roasted vegetables or as a wholesome base for plant-based protein. Its bright, zesty notes make it ideal for any season, and it's easy to customize with your favorite herbs or nuts for added texture. A simple yet elegant choice, this recipe is a sustainable and satisfying addition to your meal rotation!

PREPARATION

- Rinse wild rice thoroughly under cold water and set aside.
- Mince garlic finely to release its flavor.
- Add wild rice, garlic, olive oil, thyme, and 2 cups water to the crock pot.
- Stir gently to ensure all ingredients are evenly combined.
- Cook on low heat for 4 hours, stirring occasionally to prevent sticking.
- Stir in orange zest during the last 10 minutes of cooking to retain its vibrant aroma.
- Serve warm, garnished with additional thyme and a drizzle of olive oil.

NUTRITION

Calories, 180; Protein, 5g; Total Fat, 7g; Saturated Fat, 1g; Monounsaturated Fat, 5g; Polyunsaturated Fat, 1g; Carbohydrates, 26g; Fiber, 3g; Sugars, 1g; Added Sugars, 0g; Net Carbs, 23g; Sodium, 50mg; Potassium, 150mg; Calcium, 20mg; Iron, 1mg; Magnesium, 40mg; Vitamin A, 50 IU; Vitamin C, 5mg; Vitamin D, 0 IU; Vitamin E, 1mg; Vitamin K, 10mcg; Omega-3, 0.05g; Omega-6, 0.1g; Cholesterol, 0mg. Dietary Suitability: gluten-free, vegan. Allergen Information: none.

Braised Artichokes

INGREDIENTS

- 4 artichoke hearts
- 2 cloves garlic
- 1 tbsp lemon juice
- 1 tbsp olive oil
- 2 tbsp chopped parsley

WHY IS IT GREAT?

Braised Artichokes are a deliciously healthy dish packed with nutrients and flavor! Artichokes provide dietary fiber and antioxidants, supporting digestion and heart health. Lemon and parsley add a refreshing touch while contributing anti-inflammatory and immune-boosting benefits. Garlic and olive oil enhance the Mediterranean flavor profile and bring heart-healthy fats to the table. Cooking this recipe in a crock pot ensures the artichokes become tender and flavorful with minimal effort, making it perfect for busy schedules. Serve them as an appetizer, side dish, or light meal. This sustainable, plant-based recipe is customizable—add your favorite herbs or seasonings for extra depth. Its simplicity, nutritional value, and vibrant presentation make it a standout choice for any occasion!

PREPARATION

- Trim artichokes, removing tough outer leaves and slicing into halves.
- Mince garlic finely to release its aroma and flavor.
- Add artichokes, garlic, olive oil, and 1/4 cup water to the crock pot.
- Drizzle with lemon juice and sprinkle parsley over the top.
- Stir gently to coat artichokes with the mixture and cook on low heat for 4 hours.
- Check tenderness and adjust seasoning with more lemon juice or salt if needed.
- Serve warm, garnished with parsley and a drizzle of olive oil.

NUTRITION

Calories, 130; Protein, 3g; Total Fat, 7g; Saturated Fat, 1g; Monounsaturated Fat, 5g; Polyunsaturated Fat, 1g; Carbohydrates, 15g; Fiber, 7g; Sugars, 1g; Added Sugars, 0g; Net Carbs, 8g; Sodium, 150mg; Potassium, 350mg; Calcium, 40mg; Iron, 2mg; Magnesium, 30mg; Vitamin A, 100 IU; Vitamin C, 10mg; Vitamin D, 0 IU; Vitamin E, 1mg; Vitamin K, 15mcg; Omega-3, 0.05g; Omega-6, 0.1g; Cholesterol, 0mg. Dietary Suitability: gluten-free, vegan. Allergen Information: none.

Quinoa Salad

INGREDIENTS

- 1 cup cooked quinoa
- 1/2 cup chickpeas
- 2 tbsp chopped parsley
- 1 tbsp olive oil
- 1 tbsp lemon juice

WHY IS IT GREAT?

Quinoa Salad is a refreshing and protein-packed dish, perfect for a quick, healthy meal. Quinoa is a complete protein and rich in fiber, making it a satisfying and nutritious base. Chickpeas add additional plant-based protein and a creamy texture, while parsley and lemon juice bring anti-inflammatory and antioxidant benefits. Olive oil enhances the dish with heart-healthy fats and a smooth, rich flavor. The crock pot method ensures quinoa is cooked to perfection and allows the ingredients to meld together effortlessly. Serve this salad warm or chilled as a main dish or a side for grilled vegetables or tofu. It's versatile, customizable, and environmentally friendly, using sustainable ingredients. The bright flavors and minimal prep make it a go-to for any occasion!

PREPARATION

- Rinse quinoa and cook it in the crock pot with 2 cups of water for 2 hours on low heat.
- Drain and rinse chickpeas thoroughly under cold water.
- Once quinoa is tender, stir in chickpeas, olive oil, and lemon juice for even flavor distribution.
- Add chopped parsley and mix gently to combine.
- Taste and adjust seasoning if needed with more lemon juice or salt.
- Let the salad sit in the crock pot for an additional 15 minutes on warm to absorb flavors.
- Serve warm or at room temperature, garnished with fresh parsley and a drizzle of olive oil.

NUTRITION

Calories, 250; Protein, 8g; Total Fat, 8g; Saturated Fat, 1g; Monounsaturated Fat, 6g; Polyunsaturated Fat, 1g; Carbohydrates, 35g; Fiber, 6g; Sugars, 1g; Added Sugars, 0g; Net Carbs, 29g; Sodium, 150mg; Potassium, 400mg; Calcium, 30mg; Iron, 2.5mg; Magnesium, 60mg; Vitamin A, 200 IU; Vitamin C, 5mg; Vitamin D, 0 IU; Vitamin E, 1mg; Vitamin K, 15mcg; Omega-3, 0.05g; Omega-6, 0.1g; Cholesterol, 0mg. Dietary Suitability: gluten-free, vegan. Allergen Information: none.

Stuffed Mushrooms

INGREDIENTS

- 6 large mushrooms
- 1/2 cup cooked quinoa
- 2 cloves garlic
- 1 tbsp olive oil
- 2 tbsp chopped parsley

WHY IS IT GREAT?

Stuffed Mushrooms are a delightful and nutritious dish, perfect for any occasion! Mushrooms offer a meaty texture and are rich in vitamins D and B-complex, while quinoa provides plant-based protein and essential amino acids. Garlic and parsley add anti-inflammatory and antioxidant benefits, and olive oil enhances the dish with healthy fats. Cooking these mushrooms in a crock pot ensures they become tender and infused with the savory stuffing flavors. Serve them as an appetizer, side dish, or light main course. The recipe is highly customizable—add nuts, dried fruits, or different herbs to suit your taste. With its blend of earthy, fresh, and zesty notes, this sustainable, plant-based dish is as visually appealing as it is delicious and easy to prepare!

PREPARATION

- Clean mushrooms, remove stems, and hollow out caps for stuffing.
- Cook quinoa as per instructions and let it cool.
- Mince garlic finely and mix it with quinoa, parsley, and olive oil to create the stuffing.
- Fill each mushroom cap generously with the quinoa mixture and arrange in the crock pot.
- Drizzle with additional olive oil and cook on low heat for 3 hours.
- Check mushrooms for tenderness and adjust seasoning if necessary.
- Serve warm, garnished with parsley and a drizzle of olive oil.

NUTRITION

Calories, 180; Protein, 7g; Total Fat, 7g; Saturated Fat, 1g; Monounsaturated Fat, 5g; Polyunsaturated Fat, 1g; Carbohydrates, 22g; Fiber, 4g; Sugars, 2g; Added Sugars, 0g; Net Carbs, 18g; Sodium, 100mg; Potassium, 450mg; Calcium, 20mg; Iron, 2mg; Magnesium, 40mg; Vitamin A, 100 IU; Vitamin C, 5mg; Vitamin D, 5 IU; Vitamin E, 1mg; Vitamin K, 15mcg; Omega-3, 0.05g; Omega-6, 0.1g; Cholesterol, 0mg. Dietary Suitability: gluten-free, vegan. Allergen Information: none.

Spiced Chickpeas

INGREDIENTS

- 1 cup cooked chickpeas
- 1 tsp cumin
- 1 tsp paprika
- 1 tbsp olive oil
- 1 tbsp lemon juice

WHY IS IT GREAT?

Spiced Chickpeas are a protein-rich and flavorful dish, perfect for snacking or as a versatile side. Chickpeas are an excellent source of fiber, plant-based protein, and essential minerals, while cumin and paprika bring warmth and anti-inflammatory benefits. Olive oil adds heart-healthy fats, and lemon juice enhances the dish with a zesty finish. Cooking them in a crock pot ensures the spices fully infuse the chickpeas, creating a savory and satisfying dish with minimal effort. Serve them as a topping for salads, inside wraps, or as a standalone appetizer. The recipe is eco-friendly, affordable, and easy to customize with additional spices or herbs. Its hearty yet light profile makes it a go-to dish for any time of the day!

PREPARATION

- Rinse chickpeas thoroughly if using canned or soak and cook dried chickpeas.
- Add chickpeas, cumin, paprika, and olive oil to the crock pot.
- Stir gently to coat chickpeas evenly with the spices.
- Cook on low heat for 2 hours, stirring occasionally to enhance flavor absorption.
- Drizzle lemon juice over chickpeas in the final 10 minutes and stir well.
- Check seasoning and adjust with salt or extra lemon juice as needed.
- Serve warm, garnished with fresh parsley and a drizzle of olive oil.

NUTRITION

Calories, 220; Protein, 8g; Total Fat, 8g; Saturated Fat, 1g; Monounsaturated Fat, 6g; Polyunsaturated Fat, 1g; Carbohydrates, 30g; Fiber, 6g; Sugars, 2g; Added Sugars, 0g; Net Carbs, 24g; Sodium, 100mg; Potassium, 300mg; Calcium, 40mg; Iron, 2.5mg; Magnesium, 50mg; Vitamin A, 200 IU; Vitamin C, 5mg; Vitamin D, 0 IU; Vitamin E, 1mg; Vitamin K, 5mcg; Omega-3, 0.05g; Omega-6, 0.1g; Cholesterol, 0mg. Dietary Suitability: gluten-free, vegan. Allergen Information: none.

Turmeric Hummus

INGREDIENTS

- 1 cup cooked chickpeas
- 2 tbsp tahini
- 1 tsp turmeric
- 1 clove garlic
- 1 tbsp olive oil

WHY IS IT GREAT?

Turmeric Hummus is a creamy, nutritious delight infused with vibrant flavors and anti-inflammatory properties! Chickpeas are packed with protein and fiber, while tahini adds a nutty richness and essential healthy fats. Turmeric enhances the dish with its golden hue and potent health benefits, including reducing inflammation and boosting immunity. The crock pot method gently infuses the flavors, making this hummus irresistibly smooth and flavorful with minimal effort. Serve it as a dip with vegetables, spread on wraps, or pair with pita bread for a versatile, satisfying snack or side. Its plant-based ingredients make it eco-friendly and suitable for various dietary needs. Easy to prepare and customize, this recipe is a must-try for anyone seeking a delicious and wholesome Mediterranean-inspired dish!

PREPARATION

- Add chickpeas, tahini, minced garlic, turmeric, and 1/4 cup water to the crock pot.
- Drizzle olive oil over the ingredients and stir to combine.
- Cook on low heat for 2 hours to meld the flavors and soften the chickpeas further.
- Transfer the mixture to a blender or food processor and blend until smooth.
- Return the hummus to the crock pot and keep warm for 10 minutes.
- Adjust seasoning with salt or lemon juice if needed before serving.
- Serve garnished with a drizzle of olive oil and a sprinkle of turmeric.

NUTRITION

Calories, 220; Protein, 8g; Total Fat, 10g; Saturated Fat, 1.5g; Monounsaturated Fat, 7g; Polyunsaturated Fat, 1.5g; Carbohydrates, 26g; Fiber, 6g; Sugars, 2g; Added Sugars, 0g; Net Carbs, 20g; Sodium, 150mg; Potassium, 300mg; Calcium, 40mg; Iron, 2.5mg; Magnesium, 50mg; Vitamin A, 100 IU; Vitamin C, 5mg; Vitamin D, 0 IU; Vitamin E, 1mg; Vitamin K, 5mcg; Omega-3, 0.05g; Omega-6, 0.15g; Cholesterol, 0mg. Dietary Suitability: gluten-free, vegan. Allergen Information: contains sesame (tahini).

Marinated Olives

INGREDIENTS

- 1 cup olives
- 1 tbsp lemon juice
- 1 clove garlic
- 1 tbsp olive oil
- 1 tsp thyme

WHY IS IT GREAT?

Marinated Olives are a simple yet flavorful dish, perfect as a snack, appetizer, or addition to meals. Olives are rich in heart-healthy monounsaturated fats and antioxidants, while garlic and thyme add anti-inflammatory and immune-boosting benefits. Lemon juice enhances the tangy profile and adds a refreshing citrus note, making the dish bright and zesty. The crock pot method gently warms the olives, infusing them with the marinade for a deeply satisfying flavor. Serve these olives with crusty bread, cheese, or alongside roasted vegetables for a versatile, crowd-pleasing option. This sustainable, plant-based recipe is easy to prepare, customizable with herbs like rosemary or basil, and ideal for any occasion. You'll love how effortlessly delicious it is!

PREPARATION

- Rinse olives to remove excess brine and set aside.
- Slice garlic thinly to release its flavor.
- Add olives, garlic, olive oil, lemon juice, and thyme to the crock pot.
- Stir gently to coat olives evenly with the marinade ingredients.
- Cook on low heat for 1 hour to allow the flavors to meld together.
- Stir occasionally and adjust seasoning with additional lemon juice if desired.
- Serve warm or at room temperature, garnished with fresh thyme and a drizzle of olive oil.

NUTRITION

Calories, 150; Protein, 1g; Total Fat, 15g; Saturated Fat, 2g; Monounsaturated Fat, 12g; Polyunsaturated Fat, 1g; Carbohydrates, 2g; Fiber, 1g; Sugars, 0g; Added Sugars, 0g; Net Carbs, 1g; Sodium, 500mg; Potassium, 30mg; Calcium, 20mg; Iron, 0.5mg; Magnesium, 5mg; Vitamin A, 50 IU; Vitamin C, 2mg; Vitamin D, 0 IU; Vitamin E, 1mg; Vitamin K, 2mcg; Omega-3, 0.05g; Omega-6, 0.1g; Cholesterol, 0mg. Dietary Suitability: gluten-free, vegan. Allergen Information: none.

Eggplant Dip

INGREDIENTS

- 1 medium eggplant
- 1 clove garlic
- 1 tbsp olive oil
- 1 tbsp lemon juice
- 1 tbsp tahini

WHY IS IT GREAT?

Eggplant Dip is a smoky, creamy, and healthy dish that's perfect as a dip, spread, or side. Eggplants are low in calories but rich in antioxidants and fiber, making them excellent for digestion and heart health. Garlic and tahini add depth, while lemon juice provides a zesty balance and enhances the dip's anti-inflammatory properties. Olive oil brings richness and heart-healthy fats, completing the dish's flavor profile. The crock pot method is ideal for slow-roasting the eggplant, yielding a soft texture and deep flavor with minimal effort. Serve this dip with pita, fresh veggies, or as a spread for wraps. It's versatile, eco-friendly, and easy to customize with spices like cumin or paprika for an extra kick. Enjoy its rustic charm and wholesome taste!

PREPARATION

- Wash the eggplant and prick it with a fork for even cooking.
- Place the eggplant in the crock pot along with garlic and 1/4 cup water.
- Drizzle olive oil over the eggplant and cook on low heat for 4 hours until tender.
- Scoop out the eggplant flesh and blend it with garlic, lemon juice, and tahini until smooth.
- Return the dip to the crock pot on warm for 15 minutes.
- Adjust seasoning with salt or more lemon juice if needed.
- Serve warm or at room temperature, garnished with olive oil and parsley.

NUTRITION

Calories, 130; Protein, 2g; Total Fat, 9g; Saturated Fat, 1.5g; Monounsaturated Fat, 6g; Polyunsaturated Fat, 1g; Carbohydrates, 11g; Fiber, 4g; Sugars, 4g; Added Sugars, 0g; Net Carbs, 7g; Sodium, 50mg; Potassium, 250mg; Calcium, 20mg; Iron, 0.5mg; Magnesium, 15mg; Vitamin A, 50 IU; Vitamin C, 5mg; Vitamin D, 0 IU; Vitamin E, 1mg; Vitamin K, 5mcg; Omega-3, 0.05g; Omega-6, 0.1g; Cholesterol, 0mg. Dietary Suitability: gluten-free, vegan. Allergen Information: contains sesame (tahini).

Spiced Nuts

INGREDIENTS

- 1/2 cup almonds
- 1/2 cup walnuts
- 1/2 tsp cinnamon
- 1 tbsp olive oil
- 1 tbsp honey

WHY IS IT GREAT?

Spiced Nuts are a delightful blend of sweet and savory, perfect for snacking or entertaining! Almonds and walnuts are nutrient-dense, providing healthy fats, protein, and antioxidants that support heart and brain health. Cinnamon adds a touch of warmth and boosts metabolism, while honey provides natural sweetness and energy. Olive oil ensures the nuts achieve a glossy caramelization, and the crock pot method makes the process hands-off and hassle-free. Serve these nuts as a party snack, salad topping, or gift in decorative jars. Customize with your favorite spices like nutmeg or ginger for variety. Their anti-inflammatory properties and wholesome ingredients make them a guilt-free treat, ideal for anyone looking for a healthy and satisfying bite!

PREPARATION

- Combine almonds and walnuts in the crock pot for even coating.
- Mix olive oil, honey, and cinnamon in a small bowl until smooth.
- Pour the mixture over the nuts and stir well to coat evenly.
- Cook on low heat for 2 hours, stirring occasionally to prevent sticking.
- Check for doneness and caramelization in the final 30 minutes.
- Let the nuts cool slightly before serving for crisp texture.
- Serve warm or store in an airtight container for later.

NUTRITION

Calories, 250; Protein, 5g; Total Fat, 20g; Saturated Fat, 2g; Monounsaturated Fat, 15g; Polyunsaturated Fat, 3g; Carbohydrates, 14g; Fiber, 3g; Sugars, 9g; Added Sugars, 5g; Net Carbs, 11g; Sodium, 5mg; Potassium, 150mg; Calcium, 40mg; Iron, 1mg; Magnesium, 40mg; Vitamin A, 0 IU; Vitamin C, 0mg; Vitamin D, 0 IU; Vitamin E, 2mg; Vitamin K, 1mcg; Omega-3, 0.1g; Omega-6, 2g; Cholesterol, 0mg. Dietary Suitability: gluten-free. Allergen Information: contains nuts.

Zucchini Fritters

INGREDIENTS

- 1 medium zucchini
- 1 egg
- 1 clove garlic
- 1 tbsp olive oil
- 1 tbsp chopped parsley

WHY IS IT GREAT?

Zucchini Fritters are a delightful blend of flavor and nutrition, making them perfect for any meal or snack. Zucchini is rich in water content and nutrients like potassium and vitamin C, promoting hydration and immunity. Garlic and parsley add anti-inflammatory benefits, while eggs and olive oil contribute healthy fats and protein for a balanced dish. Cooking these fritters in a crock pot ensures they stay moist while developing a golden crust without excess oil. This method also simplifies cleanup and preparation. Serve them as a side dish, snack, or light main course. Their adaptability makes them a favorite —add cheese, herbs, or spices for variety. Easy, healthy, and visually appealing, these fritters are a must-try!

PREPARATION

- Grate zucchini and squeeze out excess water using a clean cloth.
- Mix zucchini, beaten egg, minced garlic, and parsley in a bowl until combined.
- Form small fritters and place them in the crock pot, layering with parchment paper if needed.
- Drizzle olive oil over the fritters to enhance browning.
- Cook on high heat for 2.5 hours, flipping halfway through for even cooking.
- Check for a golden crust before removing from the crock pot.
- Serve warm with extra parsley and a lemon wedge garnish.

NUTRITION

Calories, 140; Protein, 5g; Total Fat, 9g; Saturated Fat, 1.5g; Monounsaturated Fat, 6g; Polyunsaturated Fat, 1g; Carbohydrates, 10g; Fiber, 2g; Sugars, 2g; Added Sugars, 0g; Net Carbs, 8g; Sodium, 50mg; Potassium, 300mg; Calcium, 20mg; Iron, 1mg; Magnesium, 15mg; Vitamin A, 200 IU; Vitamin C, 10mg; Vitamin D, 20 IU; Vitamin E, 1mg; Vitamin K, 15mcg; Omega-3, 0.05g; Omega-6, 0.1g; Cholesterol, 50mg. Dietary Suitability: gluten-free. Allergen Information: contains eggs.

Weekly MEAL PLAN

	BREAKFAST	LUNCH	DINNER	SNACKS
MON	Lemon-Blueberry Oatmeal	Mediterranean Lentil Soup	Lemon Dill Salmon	Marinated Olives
TUE	Sweet Potato and Turmeric Hash	Tomato and Basil Soup	Chicken Gyros Bowl	Zucchini Fritters
WED	Mediterranean Veggie Frittata	Chickpea and Spinach Stew	Turmeric and Ginger Chicken	Spiced Nuts
THU	Golden Quinoa Breakfast Bowl	Butternut Squash and Ginger Soup	Cod with Tomatoes and Olives	Quinoa Salad
FRI	Golden Millet Porridge	Sweet Potato Tagine	Seafood Paella	Eggplant Dip
SAT	Spinach and Tomato Shakshuka	Moroccan Lentil Stew	Cauliflower Masala	Stuffed Mushrooms
SUN	Zucchini and Herb Breakfast Bake	Tuscan White Bean Soup	Greek Chicken with Olives	Turmeric Hummus

Weekly MEAL PLAN 2

	BREAKFAST	LUNCH	DINNER	SNACKS
MON	Warm Pear and Walnut Compote	Moroccan Chicken	Eggplant and Chickpea Stew	Braised Artichokes
TUE	Mediterranean Veggie Frittata	Lemon Chicken Orzo Soup	Turmeric Shrimp	Spiced Chickpeas
WED	Zucchini and Herb Breakfast Bake	Cauliflower Turmeric Soup	Sweet Potato Curry	Stuffed Bell Peppers
THU	Golden Quinoa Breakfast Bowl	Leek and Artichoke Soup	Herb-Crusted Trout	Marinated Olives
FRI	Lemon-Blueberry Oatmeal	Chicken with Wild Rice	Red Pepper and Fennel Soup	Zucchini Fritters
SAT	Sweet Potato and Turmeric Hash	Turmeric Chicken Soup	Saffron Mussels	Spiced Nuts
SUN	Golden Millet Porridge	Chicken with Artichokes	White Bean Ragout	Eggplant Dip

Made in the USA
Las Vegas, NV
03 January 2025